Ancient Text, Modern World

Building a **God-Centered Worldview** in a **Me-Centered World**

GENERAL EDITOR – JONATHAN DENTON

with
Peter Beck, Michael Bryant, Dondi E. Costin, Ryan Gimple,
Edward D. Gravely, Ron Harvell, R. Allen Jackson,
Peter J. Link, Jr., Ross Parker, Benjamin B. Phillips,
Jay H. Strack, and Jonathan D. Watson

D0869223

RANDALL HOUSE
— ACADEMIC —

CONTENTS

Endorsements

"I am so grateful for Dr. Denton's tireless efforts to assemble the right contributors and produce this much-needed resource. *Ancient Text, Modern World* takes on the difficult task of applied theology affording the reader the ability to understand how holy writ connects to the grit and grind of today's challenges! This is a book needed on the shelf of every student ministry practitioner."

–Brent Crowe, vice president, Student Leadership University

"Today's young people are born into a world that deconstructs everything. Many of our foundational assumptions can't be taken for granted anymore. *Ancient Text, Modern World* addresses this deconstruction by focusing on the Constructor through His Word in ways that draw young people from today's fragmented worldview to be transformed mind, soul, and spirit by His redemptive work. Get this book. Dig into it deeply, and wrestle with its implications if you want, in this generation, to 'contend for the faith that was once for all delivered to the saints.'"

–Rick Morton, Ph.D., senior vice president of engagement, Lifeline Children's Services, co-author of *Orphanology: Awakening to Gospel-Centered Adoption and Orphan Care*, and author of *KnowOrphans: Mobilizing the Church for Global Orphanology*

"Today's youth are weary and exhausted. Studies reveal most of them think life is meaningless. Their Covid-disrupted lives remain hostage to a self-absorbed social media culture. But they are a resilient lot. All they need is someone to give them a reason to believe, to hope, for them to take up the journey.

As the title of this book promises, a God-centered focus is a way to navigate their current cultural emptiness. The truths in this book are solid, as are the thirteen leaders and teachers who write to equip those who teach and mentor today's youth.

The content of the book follows three helpful themes: the reliability and message of the Scriptures, an understanding of this current cultural moment and how the Scriptures speak into it, and a concluding section providing practical perspectives for application in education and ministry.

All the contributors are involved in the journey. They have spent their lives investing in those who will come after them, and in *Ancient Text, Modern World*, they share what has worked and what is still working. A worthy resource for today."

–William E. Brown, Ph.D., senior fellow for worldview and culture, the Colson Center for Christian Worldview

"As Christian school leaders, we are most concerned with how the culture around us is winning the souls of our students. Dr. Denton and the other authors of *Ancient Text* remind us that the only way to address the soil of hopelessness in our modern students that is producing the fruit of anxiety is to learn to be effective gardeners—understanding then preparing the soil for the seed of the Word! The information is not new, but is presented in a way that gives us hope that this generation is no harder to reach than any other in history if approached with the honest and humble desire of spiritual leaders to teach the words of Scripture that are the only truths worth building our lives on. This book will help us all to become more effective, faithful, and focused servant leaders who will trust and apply the Bible effectively to make disciples for Christ."

–J. D. Zubia, headmaster, Palmetto Christian Academy

INTRODUCTION

Jonathan D. Denton, Ph.D.

Last April, I finished a year of teaching at Charleston Southern University, in South Carolina, through the COVID-19 pandemic. We started the spring semester in January, did not take any breaks throughout the semester, and finished by the end of April. Faculty and students said our goodbyes and planned to reunite at the end of August, four months later. As a former student minister, I did not know what to do with four months of no summer activities! Luckily, my wife had plenty of plans for me to stay busy. One idea she had was that our house needed repainting ... the exterior of our house ... in Charleston, South Carolina ... in the summer. I got a quote from a painter and realized I could save $7,000 if I did it myself. So I started painting. Fortunately I had four months, because it is now a year later and I am almost finished.

One thing I did enjoy about painting was that at the end of the day I could see the work I had done. This was therapeutic after a year of having to teach to students in masks and behind screens, not knowing if any learning was happening. Without seeing their faces, it was hard to see if the lessons were connecting. By the end of the semester, I was exhausted and not sure if I had made any impact. We all have moments like this when we teach students. We passionately tell the story with all we have and sometimes it is hard to see if our students are even listening. But with painting, I would take a picture with my phone at the beginning of the day and then instantly see the difference between the picture and the house by the end of the day. It was a great feeling to see real-time results of my work.

When I first began student ministry almost twenty-five years ago, many of the students who came to our programs had the main building blocks of faith. They seemed to know at least the basic stories of the Bible, the major components of the gospel and a few spiritual disciplines. As ministers, our main task was to add to our students' knowledge of the Bible and help them in their next steps in their walks with God. If their spiritual life was a building, we simply had to add a fresh coat of paint each year. Those days are gone. In many ways, we aren't adding a fresh coat of paint because the students we minister to often don't have any sort of spiritual foundation.

A couple of generations ago, we were primarily ministering to students and families who were viewing life as "God-defined." In a God-defined world, they understood that God existed, God created, and God designed the world. Thus, our teaching focused on helping them know the God of the Bible, who they were searching for. We are now ministering to students who are immersed in a "me-defined" world. The foundation has shifted. Instead of searching for God's plan and purpose for their life, students begin with creating their identity and defining how they should live.

Another thing I like to do each summer is growing fruit and vegetables. At my house, my family has several garden beds and we love to plant tomatoes, squash, watermelon, okra, and eggplants. Gardening is very different than painting. In gardening, we plant seeds into the ground and then water them for weeks and weeks before seeing any results. Even when a tomato appears, it is still several weeks before it ripens. As we minister to students today, it feels a lot more like gardening. We start from the soil up and help them to grow, often not seeing results for years. The only way to see fruit down the road is to start with the right seed. Just like we have to start with a tomato seed to grow a tomato, we have to start with the right seed to build a biblical worldview: The Word of God, our Ancient Text. As we teach the Ancient Text to a modern student, we are building a God-centered worldview in a me-centered world.

Today's headlines change as fast as the page can refresh or the feed can scroll. Yet every week, students gather in churches and Christian schools to hear teaching from a text thousands of years old. And pastors, youth ministers, small group leaders, disciplers, and teachers aim at building a God-centered worldview in their students. This book aims to present the Bible as a reliable, true, and trustworthy Ancient Text that is sufficient for ministry to a modern student with all the complexities, hurts, and mixed messages of a modern world. The focus is not only on the message that the Ancient Text gives to a modern audience but also how the Ancient Text should inform our ministry and educational practices.

This work will include three sections. The first section examines the reliability, story, and message of the Bible, our Ancient Text. The second section examines the modern world of a student and how the Ancient Text speaks into a modern world, specifically in science, education, and culture. The final section gives ministry implications of applying an Ancient Text into ministry and Christian education of a modern student. Topics in this section include developing a biblical worldview, teaching an Ancient Text, offering spiritual care to a modern student, integrating faith with education and ministry, and responding to the crises students face.

This work is a product of an apologetic conference that was created for high school students at Charleston Southern University (CSU) in the Fall of 2021. Due to a rise in COVID-19 cases in the Charleston area and cancelations of all events with visitors on CSU's campus, the conference was moved to Palmetto Christian Academy in Mount Pleasant, South Carolina for the school's upper school junior and senior students. Dr. R. Allen Jackson (senior pastor of Dunwoody Baptist Church and Professor of Youth Education and Collegiate Ministry at New Orleans Baptist Theological Seminary) and Dr. Jay Strack (founder and president of SLU) were the keynote speakers for the event around the theme of "Ancient Text Modern World." Various professors from the College of Christian Studies at CSU also presented breakouts around this theme. This conference has led to all of us coming together to write this book. I am excited for you to get to know these great professors and thought leaders as we think deeply about our Ancient Text and its message to a modern world.

About the Authors

The first section of the book focuses on the Ancient Text. The contributors to this section include R. Allen Jackson, Peter J. Link, Jr., Edward D. Gravely, Peter Beck, and Jonathan D. Watson.

R. Allen Jackson (Ph.D., New Orleans Baptist Theological Seminary) has served on the faculty of the New Orleans Baptist Theological Seminary for almost three decades. For the past several years, he has become a full-time pastor and a part time professor, serving as the senior pastor of Dunwoody Baptist Church in Atlanta, Georgia. He has written numerous articles and books. He is grateful to participate in this project with Dr. Denton, a former student.

Peter Link, Jr. (Ph.D., Southeastern Baptist Theological Seminary) has been helping churches and Christian higher education institutions to proclaim the Old Testament for over 11 years. He now serves as professor of Christians Studies at Charleston Southern University and as one of the group pastors at Crossroads Community Church in Summerville, South Carolina. He co-authored *Bible 101: From Genesis and Psalms to the Gospels and Revelation, Your Guide to the Old and New Testaments*.

Edward D. Gravely (Ph.D., Southeastern Baptist Theological Seminary) is the Ott Chair of Christian Theology and a professor of Christian Studies at Charleston Southern University. He also serves as an elder at his church in Summerville, South Carolina. He co-authored *Bible 101: From Genesis and Psalms to the Gospels and Revelation, Your Guide to the Old and New Testaments*.

Peter Beck (Ph.D., The Southern Baptist Theological Seminary) serves as professor of Christian Studies, the Ott Chair of Christian Theology, and director of the Honors Program at Charleston Southern University. In addition to his book *The Voice of Faith: Jonathan*

Edwards' Theology of Prayer, he has published numerous articles on Jonathan Edwards, the Puritans, and Baptist studies. He writes and speaks frequently on the integration of faith and learning. Additionally, Peter has more than eighteen years of pastoral experience and currently serves as lead pastor of Doorway Baptist Church in North Charleston, South Carolina.

Jonathan D. Watson (Ph.D., Southwestern Baptist Theological Seminary) is chair and associate professor of Christian Studies at Charleston Southern University. He is the author of *In the Name of Our Lord: Four Models of the Relationship Between Baptism, Catechesis, and Communion* (Lexham Academic, 2021).

The second section of the book focuses on Modern Students and Their World. The contributors to this section include another chapter from Allen Jackson as well as Ross Parker, Ryan Gimple, and Dondi E. Costin.

Ross Parker (Ph.D., Baylor University) is an associate professor of Christian Studies at Charleston Southern University where he teaches classes in Philosophy, Ethics, and Apologetics. Ryan Gimple (Ph.D., Southeastern Baptist Theological Seminary) served for 19 years as a missionary in Asia, and now teaches missions and church planting as an assistant professor of Christian Studies at Charleston Southern University.

Dondi E. Costin (Ph.D., D.Min., The Southern Baptist Theological Seminary) is a retired major general who completed his military career as U.S. Air Force chief of chaplains. He began serving as the third president of Charleston Southern University in 2018.

The final section of the book focuses on Education and Ministry to a Modern Student. The contributors to this section include Jay H. Strack, Ben Phillips, Jonathan Denton, Michael Bryant, and Ron Harvell.

For more than four decades, **Jay H. Strack** (D.Min., Luther Rice Seminary), has shared his personal story of overcoming poverty, abuse, broken homes, and drug addiction. No stranger to personal adversity, Jay believes, "There is always a way," and his life mission is to create and facilitate innovative faith-based solutions to bring about transformational leadership for this generation. He is the president and founder of Student Leadership University and founder of the Strack Center for Global Leadership and Ministry at Charleston Southern University.

Benjamin B. Phillips (Ph.D., Southwestern Baptist Theological Seminary) is the dean of the College of Christian Studies at Charleston Southern University. He has over 30 years of experience in the pulpit, having served multiple churches in Texas and South Carolina as pastor or as a preaching interim.

Jonathan D. Denton (Ph.D., New Orleans Baptist Theological Seminary) has been serving in student ministry for over 20 years, primarily in churches in South Carolina, Mississippi, and Louisiana, and is currently an associate professor of Christian Studies/Student Ministry at Charleston Southern University.

Michael Bryant (Ph.D., Southeastern Baptist Theological Seminary) has served at Charleston Southern University since 2008. He currently serves as vice president for Strategic Planning, Faith Integration, and Christian Leadership, as well as a professor of Christian Studies.

Ron Harvell, Brig. Gen. (USAF) ret., (D. Min., Southwestern Baptist Theological Seminary/Asia Graduate School of Theology) served as a chaplain missionary to the Air Force for 34 years, is now teaching on the College of Christian Studies Faculty, and is the director of Charleston Southern University's Dewey Center for Chaplaincy. He and his wife Marsha have been in 58 countries and have written six books together to help people grow in their walk with the Lord.

SECTION I

ANCIENT TEXT

In the parable of the sower, Jesus states that the "sower sows the word" (Mark 4:14, ESV). The seed that we sow to students is the Word, our Ancient Text. Two thousand years later, the seed that we sow is still the same seed. This first section will examine the reliability, story, and message of our Ancient Text. In this section, we begin with looking at the authority of our Ancient Text. We will then see the message of both the Old and New Testament. We will end with a historical look at moments when the church returned to the Bible and the importance of trusting and applying the Ancient Text.

CHAPTER 1

THE AUTHORITY OF THE ANCIENT TEXT

R. Allen Jackson, Ph.D.

Introduction

Full disclosure—I am not qualified to write about the authority of the Bible from an academic sense. Yes, I have seminary degrees, but I do not have command of the ancient languages—Greek, Hebrew, Aramaic—beyond a rudimentary level and an understanding of the tools needed to study. I am a pastor. Before that, I was a youth ministry professor. Before that, I was a youth pastor. The chapters you will read in this book are written by people who are much more qualified than me to talk about the reliability of the Ancient Text. They are smarter, have a better grasp of the ancient languages and teach it regularly. This first chapter is setting the stage for the book by introducing the basic principles needed to understand and apply the Bible.

Hopefully, what I bring to the table is a synthesis of two things that comprise my definition of what it means to embrace the authority of the Scripture, the living Word of God. First, we have to know it. Most people have never read through the entire Bible, let alone organized their study around original languages, literary

genre, word study, character study, historical context, or primary and secondary meanings of the text. So, we need to begin by
reading systematically, intentionally, and carefully. We need to take
notes, record impressions, and write down questions.

Second, we have to live it. I read a lot of books. Many of the leadership books I read prescribe or suggest a strategy, a method, or a
model. If I choose not to use that strategy and if I don't even apply
the ideas in the dreaming of my own strategy, I haven't *lived* the
book. I have taken in information, maybe even highlighted or been
impressed with an idea, the creativity, or the wordplay. I develop a
respect—or not—for the author, I investigate other books by him
or her that would be *good reading*. But if I do not implement any of
the information, I have not lived the book. I have "heard" but I have
not "listened."

Here's a funny story to help illustrate this point:

> A brand-new pastor was called to his first church. Instead of it
> being a time of excitement, it was filled with immense stress.
> He did not get the typical honeymoon that new pastors experi-
> ence. In his first month, he officiated eight funerals of church
> members. He experienced problem after problem with people,
> the church building, staff members and key volunteers resign-
> ing! He was so busy handling issues, that he didn't have time
> to work on his sermons. So this new pastor kept preaching the
> same sermon each week. After the fourth Sunday of the same
> sermon, the church council met with the bishop to complain
> about the pastor's laziness by not preparing to preach and hav-
> ing the gall to preach the same sermon four Sundays in a row.
> The wise bishop asked the church council what the sermon was
> about. The funny thing was ... they could not remember! They
> scratched their heads, hemmed and hawed, but they couldn't
> remember. The bishop said, "Let him use it one more time."

If you have truly listened to the Word of God, but have not reor-
dered your life around the commands, instructions, and guidelines,

do you truly value the Scripture? Would you say it has authority in your life? There is another old preacher story about a preacher who preached on the Great Commandment from Mark 12:28-31 to love God and love your neighbor. *He said:*

One of the teachers came to Jesus and asked Him which commandment was greatest. His reply was brilliant. You know this. "The first is, 'Hear, O Israel: the Lord our God, the Lord is one; you shall love the Lord your God with all your heart, and with all your soul, and with all your mind, and with all your strength.' The second is this, 'You shall love your neighbor as yourself.' There is no other commandment greater than these."

Like the preacher in the earlier story, he also preached the same sermon each week. Every single week he preached on the Lord's command for us to love God with everything we are and love our neighbor as ourselves. The church leaders asked him if he was too busy to write another sermon. They even offered to help with weekly ministry tasks so he could write new sermons. He replied to them, "I have plenty of time to write new sermons and I'll write one when you do what this one told you to do."

Before I move on to the part of this chapter where we dive into the authority of the Word of God, we have to have a little talk with Jesus about our personal view of the authority of the Word of God. Have we read it? Have we lived it?

Authority of Scripture

What about all the *words* that are used to describe the Bible? Is there a difference between embracing the Bible's *authority, reliability, historicity,* and *infallibility*? There are various vocabulary words to digest when beginning to take seriously the authority of the Bible. In research, particularly in social sciences, we use the terms *reliability* and *validity*. *Reliability* means that results are consistent over time. If you take a personality test and it tells you the same thing when you take it a couple more times, it is reliable. A test is *valid* if it measures what it is supposed to measure. I would argue that the Bible is both *reliable* and *valid*. It does what it is supposed to do—it is a record of God's truth as opposed to man's truth. And, over time, the words of Scripture have provided the same guidance, instruction, and inspiration as when they were written.

Bible scholars say we must embrace the historicity of Scripture. Historicity is trying to separate fact from fiction, legend from actual events. The Bible is a spiritual history of God's interaction with His people, and some would associate it with fables, and stories that were created to explain things that had happened within a specific culture. We embrace the *veracity* of the Bible in that it is an accurate representation of what God said, divinely preserved over time. We observe the *unity* of Scripture as it is a unique mesh of writing over dozens of authors over thousands of years. Primary in our approach to reading and living the Scripture is to acknowledge its truth. It is an objective and unchanging body of instruction, historical narrative, and prophecy concerning the spiritual future of the world.

In recent years, the terms *infallibility* and *inerrancy* have been used as well to address the issue of divine inspiration of Scripture. I haven't talked about that because I accept that the Bible was written by the pen of man under the inspiration of the Holy Spirit. Many articles dive into that, but it is a bit off topic for us. I do like the *Blue Letter Bible* article on the nuance between *infallibility* and *inerrancy*:

> There are two theological terms that are often used to explain the nature of the Bible—inerrancy and infallibility. They are used to point out how the Bible is different from all other books that have ever been written. Many use these terms interchangeably. Infallibility means incapable of making a mistake, while inerrancy means the absence of any error.... When referring to Scripture, the term infallible is usually used to mean reliable and trustworthy. It refers to something that is without any type of defect whatsoever. Those who trust its infallible teachings will never be lead astray. The term, "inerrancy" is more recent. While some Christians use inerrancy and infallible interchange-

> ably, they are normally used in slightly different ways. Inerrancy contends that the Bible does not have any errors of fact or any statements that are contradictory. Inerrancy is more concerned with the details of Scripture.[1]

I acknowledge these are important discussions, but many high school students may not need to go this deep. Above all else, when trying to understand the Bible, we must study it, memorize it, parse it, teach it. We confess the Bible's reliability in that it is what it claims to be over time. It claims to be inspired, the very words of God. As one writer said, "And he has spoken. The God of heaven and earth has 'forfeited his own personal privacy' to reveal himself to us—to befriend us—through a book. Scripture is like an all-access pass into the revealed mind and will of God."[2]

Paul says in 2 Timothy, "All Scripture is God-breathed and is useful for teaching, rebuking, correcting and training in righteousness, so that the servant of God may be thoroughly equipped for every good work" (2 Timothy 3:16–17, NIV). God-breathed is one of my most favorite metaphors in all of Scripture because it makes me think of a Father who breathed life into Creation and then breathed life into the written words that would guide, confront, console, and encourage us. God inspired men to write the Bible.

In John 17:17 Jesus was pouring into His disciples for one of the last times before He was crucified. He prayed for them—and us—with a lengthy prayer that is profound in its simplicity and promise. Jesus prayed to the Father for the disciples to be sanctified in the truth, set apart and made holy unto Him.

"Sanctify them in the truth; your word is truth" (John 17:17, ESV).

---

[1] Don Stewart. *What Is the Difference Between the Inerrancy of Scripture and the Infallibility of Scripture?* Retrieved from https://www.blueletterbible.org/Comm/stewart_don/faq/bible-difficulties/question5-difference-between-inerrancy-infallibility.cfm.

[2] Matt Smethurst. *8 Things Your Bible Says About Itself.* (29 July, 2020) Retrieved from https://www.thegospelcoalition.org/article/bible-says-about-itself/.

Jesus prayed that they would be set apart for God, but the basis of that consecration was the truth of God's Word. Jesus knew the Bible was absolutely true and will affect a person who internalizes the Word. **But if we aren't convinced of the authority of it, it is just an academic exercise.**

This past summer, our youth pastor invited me to speak to the students at camp. I wanted to tell them how I pray for them, so I picked a verse among many verses to set up my talk. I introduced my comments with the passage from Joshua 3 where the not-so-confident heir to the leadership of the Hebrew nation ("after the death of Moses") was trying to speak courage into the people. God had to tell him multiple times to "be strong and courageous" so he was either in *fake 'til you make it mode* or he had a word from God. He told them, "Consecrate yourselves for tomorrow the LORD will do amazing things among you" (Joshua 3:5b, NIV). Then I told them that to consecrate themselves was to make themselves available to what God wanted to do with their lives and I concluded with a prayer. You probably heard the same prayer from your pastor or youth pastor, but I'll pray it over you anyway because it fits with why you are here.

I pray that by the time you graduate from high school ...

> You will be able to recognize and respond to the lordship of Christ
>
> You will prioritize honoring God above pleasing people.
>
> You will know your way around the Bible, and know how to study it on your own
>
> You will discover and practice spiritual disciplines
>
> You will develop and demonstrate Christ's character to others
>
> You will consider God as you make wise decisions
>
> You will prioritize godly relationships
>
> You will make an intentional impact on others.

I get pretty passionate about the connection between critical thought and spiritually healthy young adults. I want you guys to have success by every measure as you make your way into college and beyond. I want you to be able to think for yourself and respect-fully challenge things you hear from other students and even fac-ulty based on the foundation that is being laid. My passion got my feelings hurt. A couple of the adult volunteers, after hearing me talk to the students at camp said to me, "You should preach like that all the time." Hurtful but correct. We should be so motivated by our love for people and our love for God and our commitment to His Word that we have a sense of urgency all the time. Otherwise, it is just academic.

I have made some assumptions. I assume you believe that the Bible is important and you accept that God is God and you are not. I also assume you affirm the authority of the Word of God, but that is really what I want to talk about this morning. I borrow again from Matt Smethurst who said, "As countercultural and counterintuitive as it may feel, submission to God's Word is where true life and free-dom are found."[3]

Definitions

In addition to the terms used to describe the essence of the Bi-ble, you will hear lots of other definitions, all of them essential. The English word *Bible* comes from the Greek word *byblos*, which means papyrus. Papyrus was ancient paper used to make books. Simply, *The Bible* means *the book*. For us, it refers to the collection of Jew-ish and Christian writings generally accepted as sacred Scriptures. We will also use the terms *Bible, Scripture(s), Word, and Word of God* interchangeably because they all refer to the same God-breathed book.

Those who wrote the Bible in Hebrew and Greek understood that written language was powerful. Words have meaning. Language shapes culture. They understood the Word of God to be more than

---

[3] Matt Smethurst. *8 Things Your Bible Says About Itself.* (29 July, 2020) Retrieved from https://www.thegospelcoalition.org/article/bible-says-about-itself/.

writing on a page. The Word was personal, interactive, and alive. Both the Word Incarnate (Jesus Christ) and the Word of God (the Bible) were sent by God to reveal Himself, His character, and His purpose.

You will hear the word, *canon* which deals with how it was decided that the books we have in our Bible are the right ones, how they came to be in our Bible. You will hear the term, *inspiration*. The New Testament writers assumed the inspiration of the Old Testament and we assume the inspiration of all biblical writers. In other words, God actually enlightened the writers as to what to write. See 2 Timothy 3:16.

You will hear about the *uniqueness* of the Bible—the continuity, the consistency, the preservation, the distinctive fit across all the Bible's writers and all the centuries. You will deal with the *authenticity* of the Bible. Many religions assume the authenticity of the Old Testament, but it is the New Testament which is a source of contention because of its narrow view of salvation.

Christianity is a historical religion, concerned with what God in Christ has actually done. The New Testament is the written account of what the eyewitnesses saw and heard, while God continues to guide believers through prayer and the leading of the Holy Spirit, the Scripture is our basis for understanding God's will for us. God will never direct us to do anything contrary to His written Word.

The Bible is divided into two sections: Old Testament and New Testament. The word *testament* makes us think of writing a legal will, a last will and testament—a document that legally directs what happens to our stuff when we die. In both the Greek and Hebrew, however, the idea is in the words *settlement, treaty,* or *covenant.* I like the last one best and it is probably the best word picture. A *covenant* is a promise between people. The Old Testament and the New Testament represent the Old Covenant and the New Covenant between God and His people. A covenant has no authority unless the parties agree to stick to it. Oddly, the only motivator for keeping a covenant is love.

I made a covenant with my wife almost 40 years ago that I would love her in sickness and in health, for richer for poorer, for better for worse, forsaking all others 'til death do us part. As we will discuss much more later, the marriage covenant has become pretty disposable in our culture. When the love breaks down, the covenant breaks down, but when we love and are loved, the covenant is robust. The covenant has authority in that it guides how I think, how I feel and what I do.

Authority comes in different ways. A conquering army can demand submission as in the Roman or Ottoman Empire. Authority can be voluntary—you get a job and with it you get a boss. Authority can be granted willingly as you realize that the person or thing to which you submit is a better, higher, nobler way. To grant someone or something authority is to admit that you are better off under the guidance or power of that person or thing.

We submit to God and what He has said (the Scriptures). Of course, we who are God-lovers and Christ-followers ultimately submit to God, not out of coercion or force, but because we have seen that it is a better way. The way of faith has experiential validity—for millennia people have seen that it works. It also has what researchers call *reliability*. In statistics, reliability says that a test measures what it says it will measure. In faith, we give authority to the Bible because it is reliable. When God's Word recorded prophecies, they were fulfilled.

This brings us to apologetics. *Apologetics* is literally, a verbal defense or a speech in defense of what one has done or a truth of which one believes. It comes from Greek word, *apologia* which means defense. In 1 Peter 3:15-16,

> But in your hearts set revere Christ as Lord. Always be prepared to give an answer to everyone who asks you to give the reason for the hope that you have. But do this with gentleness and respect, keeping a clear conscience, so that those who

speak maliciously against your good behavior in Christ may be ashamed of their slander (NIV).

For now, permit me to define apologetics as meaning that we employ *critical thinking* to work out our faith. We will separate emotion from evidence—I'll talk more about that later—and we will carefully examine the Ancient Text, compare it with what contemporary society calls *news* or *fact,* and hopefully grant authority—personally and passionately—to the words of the text, and more importantly to the One who inspired their writing.

One aspect of critical thinking is to study it systematically and not just randomly. Two of many approaches are *inductive* and *deductive* study of the text. Deductive study is like Sherlock Holmes. You find a clue in a verse or passage and look for the bigger meaning. Inductive study is like Google Earth. You start with a wide shot—a chapter, verse, or type of Scripture—and try to land on the guiding principle or theme.

Inductive Bible Study (inductive means "general to specific") is often described as a process of observation, interpretation, and application. The reader observes the structure, the big picture, determines word meanings, time frames, geographical locations, and people relationships, the author and audience, the type of Scripture and the text itself. An attempt is made to interpret how all of these observations point to a meaning or interpretation. Finally, a conclusion is suggested as to what persons should think, do, or feel as a result of understanding the text more clearly.

Deductive Bible Study (deductive means specific to general) usually begins from a pre-assigned point—a verse or a topic to investigate, and then examines the Scripture in a widening arc to determine the instruction or conclusion from the Bible regarding the inquiry. Deductive Bible study provides general principles regarding a specific point. It is probably the most well-known and used technique in pastoral ministry. For example, I might read the shortest verse in the Bible, John 11:35 and ask, "Why did Jesus weep?" As I widened my search, I would discover His love for a friend who had died as well as a passion for people who did not understand the gospel.

Living It: How We Really Embrace the Authority of Scripture

I have been in the world of academia for well over four decades as a student and professor. Whenever I take a personality test or a gifts assessment, I always score high on any category associated with teaching. I remember graduating from seminary with my master's degree and having a very real, very profound sense from God that I would return there to teach one day. Another degree and a decade later, I had the honor of taking my place on the faculty of the New Orleans Baptist Theological Seminary.

When I returned to the local church as a senior pastor with the responsibility of preaching every week, it should have surprised no one that my style was more as a teacher than as a preacher. When I first heard someone say that, I was a little hurt. Stereotypical assumptions consider preaching to be enthusiastic, even loud. Teaching can be systematic and dry. Teaching is instruction on biblical truth, and preaching is prophetic and personal. Preaching aims at the heart, but teaching aims at the head and the hands. I wanted to inspire. I wanted to be prophetic. But I loved teaching. I loved the Bible. I woke up at night trying to think of new ways to explain Scripture so that my church would grab onto the truth and the urgency and the authority of the Bible.

Walter Kaiser addresses this issue in his book on preaching and teaching:

> A gap of crisis proportions exists between the steps generally outlined in most seminary or biblical training classes in exegesis and the hard realities most pastors face every week as they prepare their sermons. Nowhere in the total curriculum of theological studies has the student been more deserted and left to his own devices than in bridging the yawning chasm between understanding the content of Scripture as it was given in the

past and proclaiming it with such relevance in the present as to produce faith life, and bona fide works.[4]

Bridging the yawning chasm between careful study and relevant application is the task of any preacher and it should be the challenge of any Christian. We need to understand the meaning of the Bible because we have recognized that it has authority in our lives. As I said before, the true test of authority is whether we live it. To live it, we have to build the bridge between analyzing the words of the Bible and understanding in plain terms what it means for us in everyday life. Preachers (*proclaimer* or *herald*) and teachers (*explainer* or *instructor*) build that bridge. Preaching is proclaiming good news to people (especially those who haven't heard it before) and teaching is explaining things about the Bible gospel that people don't understand, and helping them to live in light of it.

So, first we acknowledge its authority. Then we read it carefully, we memorize it, meditate on it. We study it inductively and deductively and use commentaries, dictionaries, and lexicons to understand the meaning of the words. We see it as literature, with books written in various genres of law, history, wisdom and poetry, prophecy, gospel, and letters. The characters, both heroic and tragic. The words of Jesus. And we build the bridge more carefully when we understand that the verses, chapters, books, and testaments are not unrelated to each other—they are tied together in the metanarrative of the Scripture.

The Bible as Metanarrative[5]

One of the ways we live the authority of Scripture is to see the Bible as a story that God wrote for us through the minds and pens of humans. When we see ourselves in the grand story of God's activ-

---

[4] Walter C. Kaiser, Jr. *Toward an Exegetical Theology: Biblical Exegesis for Preaching and Teaching*, p. 18.

[5] Adapted from R. Allen Jackson. (2015) *Disciple: The Ordinary Person's Guide to Discipling Teenagers*, chapter 3 "The DNA of Discipleship." YM360.

ity with and through His people, we might not think of submission to biblical authority as such an obligation and more of a joy. The Bible is a whole story, not a series of disconnected verses, chapters, and books. The Word is a document that God inspired to be written by humans for humans and with the understanding that humans would change over the centuries, and that humans would need the redemptive work of God throughout all of history. Unfortunately, for many readers, the Bible is just a collection of random stories or even more random verses, to be contained at church. Stepping back from the individual verses and stories, though, a continual story is apparent. The word *metanarrative* has been used to describe the *big story* or *grand narrative* of the Bible—the thread that explains and connects many little stories. The metanarrative of the Bible is the story of Jesus, God's self-revelation to the world.

A disciple should have an awareness of the whole Bible, not in a frightening way, but in a way that sees God's love and purpose whether you are reading the words of Moses, Malachi, or Matthew. *Hermeneutics* is the process of interpretation to understand what the author intended to say and what application was in view. *Exposition* is exposing the text—its language and context, in support of the author's intended purpose.

What I understand him to say is that we need to know the assumptions or rules we use to study and interpret the Bible. We assume that God inspired the Bible. We assume that God had in mind that Jesus would be sent to die for our sins. We assume that the relationship between God and man is personal. We assume that the starting point to understanding Scripture is to consider other Bible passages.

Other assumptions—the author had a clear and objective meaning and purpose in mind when recording his thoughts; the author used language and structures that were meaningful and understandable to his original intended audience; that objective meaning and purpose can be known and is anchored in history (this avoids a reader-response, subjective, and existential hermeneutic); we assume that God is consistent in character and that His character as revealed through His actions in history past (recorded in Scripture) remain consistent with contemporary circumstances. Hermeneutics is a word that describes the way theology interacts with the principles of interpreting the biblical record.

The clearly understand the Bible, we must acknowledge three challenges. First, the Old Testament was written in Hebrew and Aramaic and the New Testament was written in Greek—all foreign languages to most readers. Second, we have to struggle with how much a dynamic world impacts our study; what are the timeless principles, and what principles have to be considered in light of ever-changing culture? Finally, we remember that the events of the Bible happened thousands of years ago and over the period of several thousand years.

My point here is that we should not be intimidated by the challenges of understanding the Scripture. We should be alert for any agendas that a biblical commentator might have, but we should assume that God meant for us ordinary people to understand it. Mostly, we should approach the Bible as a whole story. Even though the types of literature represented in the Bible range from history to biography to poetry to prophecy to gospel to epistle, the Old and New Testaments come together to tell the story of God at work among men.

In 1 Corinthians 2:12-13, Paul penned, "What we have received is not the spirit of the world, but the Spirit who is from God, so that we may understand what God has freely given us. This is what we speak, not in words taught us by human wisdom but in words taught by the Spirit, explaining spiritual realities with Spirit-taught words" (NIV).

The Bible is meant to be understood and
God's story is meant to be retold.
As we find our place in God's story, we retell it by living it.

CHAPTER 2

THE STORY AND MESSAGE OF THE OLD TESTAMENT

Peter J. Link, Jr., Ph.D.

Introduction

What should Christians do with the Old Testament? It's big, a little strange at times, and very strange at others. We *know* as Christians that the Old Testament is important, but we don't know what to do with what we read. How should we respond to its lengthy law codes, boring genealogies, dramatic poems, and eerie narratives that unveil a litany of ruthless murders, horrific sexual sins, broken families, divine wrath, and national calamities? The first-time reader will be perplexed, and the long-time reader will still find himself scratching his head.

Yet, those who repeatedly jump into the Old Testament and *recognize* its larger patterns will begin to comprehend the book's big picture. They will also discover that its patterns reflect the very patterns of *our* world. The best way to apply the Ancient Text to our modern lives is not to race to our own situations after ten minutes alone with the text. Instead, we need to spend long stretches of time meditating on its words by reading, re-reading, and re-reading again. We should, in a sense, pitch a tent alongside Abraham,

Moses, and David, as they walk with God. In doing so, we will find an old story that touches every part of our modern lives. We share their pain. In Christ, we also share their hope.

In this chapter, we will learn how we can spend time in the Old Testament in order to learn that *its story is our story*. We will examine basic principles of reading the Old Testament well and then apply them to a very brief walkthrough of the Old Testament.

Principles to Reading the Old Testament Well

The Old Testament Is a Book Written to Readers (even us)

We should read the Old Testament employing four principles:

1. Keep prayerfully reading the Old Testament.
2. Remember that biblical authors anticipated readers like you.
3. Trust the design of the book as you read by reading whole books of the Old Testament.
4. Stay involved in your local church and obey what you understand.

1. *Keep prayerfully reading the Old Testament.*

When I became a Christian at the age of 31, I struggled greatly with trying to read the Old Testament. Nonetheless, in short order, I made my way into the Old Testament and began reading. I understood very little of what I read, but by God's grace I forced myself to push through that first reading. What made this first reading profitable did not appear right away. It only appeared when I *returned* to the Old Testament. In returning to the text, a reader anticipates more of the story. His prior reading has given him a *roadmap* that he continues to draw in his mind with each new reading. He is *discovering* what is there with each journey in the book because genuine understanding takes time. It, also, takes prayer. There is no way to truly understand the Old Testament apart from authentic prayer because we are called to hear *and* obey it. We must heed it *and* trust its message. Time with His Word *and* time in prayer shape good Bible reading. There are no shortcuts.

2. Remember that biblical authors anticipated readers like you.

We must not confuse where and when the Old Testament takes place, its setting, with what it teaches. The Old Testament uses the setting of the Old Covenant, the Mosaic Covenant, to convey hope in a future New Covenant. By showing us Israel's failures to approach God and live, the text teaches and reveals 1) the problem of man's death in God's presence because of our sin-filled hearts and 2) the hope of a Person, the Messiah, who will come and change man's hearts to bring man to God. Because every generation and all peoples share in this same problem and hope, the biblical authors designed their books to push through those barriers one generation at a time. They do so because everyone will need to learn what they learned. These biblical authors knew they were writing to those in their days *and* to later readers and far-away nations.

In general, people write books to preserve and pass on knowledge beyond the present moment. These authors knew that 1) many will reject God's wisdom but 2) all will need the lessons that Moses and the Prophets learned in God's presence. These two realities pressed biblical authors to craft books via divine inspiration that could endure every man's questions. They did not shy away from the brutal ugliness of this world, but they also offered future hope in God. He is their message to all readers, even us.

While biblical authors knew nothing about our smartphones, they do know who and what we need. They designed their biblical books to move past the interpretive barriers of time and place through faithful people, especially communities, who will keep talking about God's Word until the very end of time. While it is important that we not impose our modern ideas on the Ancient Text, it is equally important that we know that these books anticipate the most important aspects of our situations and compel us to not only receive the Old Testament's message but to pass it on to the next generation.

3. Trust the design of the book as you read by reading whole books of the Old Testament.

We must trust every biblical author. We need to *discover* the author's ideas as they are preserved in the text itself. If we have confidence that a Hollywood blockbuster film has an intentional design, how much more confidence should we have in the biblical text's design? Our goal with each reading should include thinking through *why* the book is shaped the way it is shaped. We discover the author's ideas by seeking *how* a biblical author designed his book. Our reading needs to also be *a faithful questioning* of why the author laid out his book as he did. We need to trust that the text is true and that it has an intelligent design. Our faithful questions emerge from asking what lesson emerges from his design, from *how* the author laid out his book. We need to ponder 1) what's included in the text, 2) what's repeated in it, and 3) what's side by side in the book. Our reading must become *a contemplative conversation* with and *a question-filled search* of the author's work and words.

If we commit to reading the whole book in this manner, we can think through *how* the author designed his book, its composition. From noticing the relationship of its beginning to its ending, we can discover which stories he set side by side and which words and situation he repeats. In searching for these features, we can recognize the book's larger patterns. These patterns draw together different parts of the book. When Isaac's story echoes Abraham's, we know that the author wants us to read these two moments together. When he sets Abraham's great victory in a battle alongside his fear of God not keeping His promise, we know that the author wants us to read these two moments together. They explain each other, highlighting the book's dilemma and hope. The book's hope becomes its lesson and message to the reader. It's what the author teaches us. God's past actions promise and foreshadow His future work. Israel's past portrays our future.[1] The book's message reaches

---

[1] John H. Sailhamer. *The Pentateuch as Narrative: A Biblical and Theological Commentary.* Zondervan, 1992.

from the Ancient Text into our present world by showing us that our flawed humanity only finds refuge in a God who can save us from our own broken hearts.

4. Stay involved in your local church and obey what you understand.

All of the other principles have focused on reading the Old Testament alone, but it is designed to be read alone *and* in community. It is meant to be read together within the church. Our reading together is not just about reading with those friends we find in our small group or local church because it also includes reading with the long tradition of faithful Christians who have passed the text to us. Good Bible reading is a community project, seeking to not only understand its message but to live it out together as well. It is only when we commit to heeding the text's main ideas that we gain the proper *posture* toward the Scripture. A right posture sets God and His text authoritatively over us. Our goal is to learn more, obey more, and trust more each day. Spending time with God in this way and with these four basic principles allows us to better understand the Old Testament's story and message.

A Brief Survey of the Old Testament

The Torah (Genesis, Exodus, Leviticus, Numbers, Deuteronomy)

While we often consider the Torah to be five books, it is truly one book in five parts with one message that emerges from how God relates to the first man, Adam, in the garden and to the nation Israel at Mt. Sinai.[2] God's Word and Spirit are present so that Adam and Israel may enjoy life with God, but neither can remain near God through a law (Adam) or series of laws (Israel). In both situations, God's judgment of their sin also manifests His mercy. He delays their deaths to give them time to repent but also acknowledges that

---

[2] Seth D. Postell. *Adam as Israel: Genesis 1–3 as the Introduction to the Torah and the Tanakh.* James Clarke and Co, 2012.

all sin must be judged in death. This delayed judgment is accompanied by the promise that the seed of the woman, a person who will come in the last days, will return man to God's presence, and defeat the work of the seed of the serpent. Moses sets us on a search for and anticipation of this seed of the woman: a prophet, priest, and king who will do what Adam could not do.

The search for the seed of the woman follows Adam's family to Abram, who is Abraham. The promised person will come through his family and will bring God's people to the land where God dwells. The land of Canaan is the promised land where God and man will dwell together, and Abraham believes that he will dwell in God's presence after his death. God tests Abraham's faith by asking him to sacrifice his own promised son, Isaac, the one whom he loves, on a mountain where God will speak to him. Upon seeing the mountain on the third day, Abraham obeys, trusts, and fears God. He takes his only son on the mountain where God dwells because he knows they will both go up, worship, *and* return. Even when he knows that his son faces death in God's presence, he also knows that God will provide a lamb in place of Isaac, to delay his death. The lamb does not show up, but God's Word delays his death and provides a substitute ram. We must wait for the lamb of God to be provided on the mount of the LORD (Genesis 22:14).

After Abraham's family finds themselves in exile in Egypt, God raises up a deliverer, Moses, who brings them out of Egypt. As Abraham approached God in a test on a mountain on the third day where his only son would die, so Moses brings Israel, God's son, to another mountain where God will speak on the third day as part of a test. Moses is asked to bring Israel on the mountain (Exodus 3:12; 19:13), but Israel trembles when God descends on the mountain (Exodus 19:16), fearing death in God's presence. In response to this disobedience, God mercifully provides His Word for Israel as part of Israel asking for God's Word so that they may stay close to God without dying in His presence. Because of God's Word, we see Israel move from a bad fear of God, which disobeyed God's voice, to a good fear of God, which draws near to Him through His Word. This

Mosaic covenant and its laws will hold Israel in place until the last days when the one promised to Abraham will arrive, when God will be on earth. Israel's time at Mt. Sinai, where God descends on it, becomes the preview of what awaits all people in the end when we die. We will see God's face. Will we live when that happens?

After Israel fails to go into the land of Canaan for the same reason they would not go on Mt. Sinai with God, God delays Israel's journey to Canaan. For the next 38 years, God tests Israel in the wilderness. It is a "slow death" for the first generation, giving them time to repent and find life by His Word in the "Torah school"[3] of life with God in the wilderness. After they die, the new generation hears Moses teach God's Word to them in three great speeches and two great poems that interpret Moses' book, the Torah. In the book's final two poems (Deuteronomy 32–33), Moses identifies the day when God descended on Mt. Sinai as a preview of what awaits all men in the end. He promises Israel will fail to follow the law codes of the Mosaic Covenant, but the person promised to Abraham, Isaac, and Jacob will come in the last days so that Israel and the nations will dwell with God as His priests in a promised land that covers the whole creation with the face of God (Genesis 49; Numbers 23–24; Deuteronomy 32–33). Moses' book ends waiting for this promised person to come. This seed of the woman promised to Adam will be a king from the tribe of Judah and a Prophet like Moses who will overcome what Adam and Moses could not overcome. He will defeat the problem of man's death in God's presence through man's death, His own death, in God's presence.

The Prophets (Joshua, Judges, 1 & 2 Samuel, 1 & 2 Kings; Isaiah, Jeremiah, Ezekiel, the 12 Minor Prophets)

The Prophets begin with the story of Israel's time in the land of Canaan with Israel starting in exile (Joshua 1) and ending in exile (2 Kings 25), as Moses wrote. God promises to be with Joshua, a

---

[3] Baal HaTurim, *Baal HaTurim Chumash: The Torah: with the Baal HaTurim's Classic Commentary Translated, Annotated, and Elucidated Vol. 5 Devarim / Deuteronomy* (2d ed.; ed. Avie Gold; trans. Eliyahu Touger; Brooklyn: Masorah Publications, 2007), 2146–7.

prophet, priest, and king, as He was with Moses through meditating on Moses' book day and night. While Joshua leads Israel into the land of Canaan well, he cannot conquer one part of the promised land: the human heart. Echoing Moses, he promises that Israel will fail to follow the law codes and find themselves in exile. After his death, Israel becomes worse than Sodom and Gomorrah. God raises up temporary deliverers, judges, who cannot stop Israel's slide and leave the reader crying out for a king who will lead Israel to do what is right in God's eyes.

The last judge, Samuel, anoints the first two kings: Saul from the tribe of Benjamin and David from the tribe of Judah. Saul's failure paves the way for David's ascension to the throne where God rejects David's good desire to build a house for God. The Son of David will be the one to build God's everlasting house. This Son of David is the same person promised to Adam and Abraham. After receiving this promise, David and his sons fail terribly. God's promise, however, remains. David's son, Solomon, and all his descendants after him fail to be the promised Son of David. After many years of sin, God exiles His people to Babylon. They must wait for the promised Son of David.

After completing this story of Israel's time in the land, the prophetic books explain why God exiled Israel. They remind readers of what God promises in the Torah. Isaiah, first, considers Moses's poems in Deuteronomy 32–33 and challenges his readers to wait for the Son of David, Immanuel, whose atoning death will bring life to His people who trust Him and will cover the whole creation with God's glory. Jeremiah, in like manner, explains how Deuteronomy 29–30 promise the great return of God's people to God in the end (Jeremiah 29–33). Ezekiel calls his readers to consider Mt. Sinai and the tabernacle from the Torah. He promises that God will change the hearts of His people so that they can live with Him forever. Then, Hosea through Malachi serve as one twelve-part book, which walks back through Israel's time in the land and offers hope for Israel and the nations when God's broken family will be restored to Him through the Son of David in the last days.

The Writings (Psalms, Job, Proverbs, Ruth, Ecclesiastes, Song of Songs, Lamentations, Esther, Daniel, Ezra Nehemiah, 1 & 2 Chronicles)

The Writings begins in Psalms with a discussion of the Blessed Man, the Son of David who meditates upon the Torah day and night (Psalm 1–2). Everything Joshua was supposed to do, this man will do. Choosing to seek refuge in Him through repentance becomes the central hope of the Psalms and a series of books that extol the surpassing value of divine wisdom over human wisdom. For Proverbs, Ruth, Song of Songs, Ecclesiastes, and Lamentations, the mercy of God shows up in waiting for this Son of David. Divine Wisdom in these books is a person who heeds the Torah and makes a path for all people to seek refuge in Him. Esther and Daniel explain God's presence by His Word in exile and the hope of what He will do in the last days. Ezra and Nehemiah show God's people returning to the dirt of Canaan, but they sin as their fathers did. The Son of David has not yet come to change their hearts. In the end, Chronicles reviews the entire Old Testament to explain how we should wait for the Son of David. The last line of the Old Testament in this three-part Hebrew order is found in 2 Chronicles 36. A Gentile king—one who should be His enemy—declares that the time is ripe for the Son of David to come and build God's house: "Let Him go up!"

Conclusion

By carefully reading the Old Testament, we can see that its message is a future hope in the person and the work of the Son of David, Christ crucified. Adam's and Israel's failures are not the end of their story with God. The time is ripe to trust the Messiah that the Old Testament promises. We better understand who He is and what He did when we wrestle with the Old Testament because Moses and the Prophets wrote to us, and they wrote to us about Jesus.

CHAPTER 3

THE STORY AND MESSAGE OF THE NEW TESTAMENT

Edward D. Gravely, Ph.D.

As Dr. Jackson explained in the close of his chapter on the "Authority of the Ancient Text," modern students face several challenges in understanding the story and message of the New Testament. In my twenty years of teaching, I have seen these challenges made all the more difficult by the way we present the Bible to them, especially the New Testament. Most students for much of their lives only read the Bible haphazardly. Even students we would consider to be diligent Bible readers rarely encounter the New Testament as it was intended to be read.

A faithful Christian student might, for example, read a paragraph from the Gospels with a devotional every morning. He or she might then hear a paragraph from an epistle on Sunday during the sermon and then study yet another paragraph from Acts on Wednesday night. Let's be honest; for most students, that is a lot of Bible in a week. The students, however, have little idea where in the Bible those paragraphs come from. They are disembodied words put under their noses, often with little context, and most students have no idea how those texts fit together into the larger story and message of the New Testament.

I firmly believe that when students are taught to read the New Testament as it was designed to be read—as one story—the story and message of the New Testament clearly emerge. I do not believe that this level of sophistication with the Bible is above the heads of average students, not if taught well. Teaching the Bible in this way, in fact, makes the New Testament far easier to understand.

The Layout of the New Testament

In our modern Bibles, the books of the New Testament are arranged as an anthology, grouped by genre and author. There is a logic and a theology to this grouping of which most readers are unaware. Making Bible readers aware of this layout, however, is crucial to them understanding what they are reading. There is a great deal of discussion among scholars as to how ancient Christians collected, circulated, and arranged the books of the New Testament, but that is a discussion for another time. The discussion here refers primarily to our modern Bibles, the Bibles students will have in their hands.

For review, consider the following: The New Testament begins with the four Gospels. This makes sense to even the casual reader; the New Testament is ultimately about Jesus, so it is fitting to begin with accounts of Jesus' birth, life, death, and resurrection, even though most of the New Testament was already written by the time the first Gospel was written.[1] From the very beginning of the life of the New Testament, Matthew has typically been the first Gospel in the collection of Gospels. Though it was almost certainly not written first (the Gospels are not in chronological order), Matthew is the Gospel that helps the reader make the most sense of Jesus in light of the Old Testament, so it sits well at the beginning of the collection of Gospels and thus between the Old Testament and the

---

[1] There is tremendous debate among scholars about the dating of the various New Testament books. Throughout this chapter, I will only refer to dates generally, using dates for the books that anyone is likely to find in any of the major New Testament surveys. Little of what I say throughout, however, hinges on any one date being correct.

rest of the New Testament.[2] Acts picks up right where the Gospels end, so putting Acts immediately following the last Gospel makes good sense.

A collection of Paul's letters follows Acts, and the second half of the book of Acts tells the history and circumstances behind the writing of most of Paul's letters. Paul's letters are grouped in modern New Testaments mostly by length, a very ancient tradition.[3] These letters explain the teaching of Jesus from the Gospels to mostly non-Jewish readers and apply the teaching of Jesus to specific circumstances that Christian churches faced then and face now.

The General Letters follow Paul's letters in modern Bibles. These are a collection of the letters that were written by other apostles and people closely connected to the apostles. These letters are grouped by author and were written throughout the second half of the first century. Much like Paul's letters, these General Letters explain the teaching of Jesus and then apply that teaching to specific circumstances that churches face. These letters also give us a look into what church life is like after the book of Acts ends.

Revelation is the last book of the New Testament. Since according to most Christian traditions Revelation describes the kingdom of God, the end of the age, and the age to come, it makes sense to most readers, modern and ancient, that Revelation should bring the New Testament and the whole Bible to a close.

Teaching the Story of the New Testament

I try to never open the Bible to teach my students without first spending some time explaining where in the New Testament we will be reading and how our text fits into the larger story and message

---

[2] Most of the earliest discussions about the Gospels by ancient Christians have Matthew listed first *because* they believed that it was the first Gospel written. Most modern scholars, however, believe that Mark was written first.

[3] Most ancient manuscript collections have Paul's letters ordered from longest to shortest, though Galatians is slightly shorter in Greek than Ephesians but comes before it. Also, the letters Paul wrote to individuals are grouped together, sorted by both recipient and length, and put at the end of the collection.

of the New Testament. I try to constantly review the layout and message of the New Testament. Students will not pick this up by osmosis. They have to be taught and modeled this approach.

For example, here is how I opened a lesson to my students just recently:

> Okay students, turn in your Bibles to 2 Thessalonians 2. We are going to be reading the first 12 verses today. But first, let's review. Second Thessalonians is one of Paul's letters, inspired by God as Holy Scripture but written by one of Jesus' earliest followers. Has everyone found it? It is in your Bible among all of Paul's other letters. Christians grouped them together to make them easy to find.
>
> Remember, Paul was a missionary and had recently visited the Thessalonians on a missionary trip. While he was there, Paul explained to them the gospel—that Jesus was the Savior God had been promising. Jesus was God in a human body, who lived a perfect life, died on the cross for the sins of the world, rose from the dead, and then sent His followers into the world to proclaim the good news to anyone who would stand still long enough to listen. Many of those Thessalonians believed in Jesus, and Paul began to teach them all the things that Jesus taught when He was here on earth. But then Paul was run out of town, leaving the Thessalonians with a bunch of questions, so Paul, under the inspiration of the Holy Spirit, wrote them this second letter. You can read about Paul's time with the Thessalonians in Acts 17—that's the book right after the four Gospels at the front of the New Testament that tells what happened right after Jesus rose from the dead. And you can read about the teaching of Jesus that Paul is referring to in 2 Thessalonians 2 in a bunch of places, but Matthew 24—the first book of the New Testament—is a great place to start if you want to hear this from Jesus himself. Don't forget the pattern of the New Testament: Jesus taught His disciples, and His disciples turned around and taught everyone else. The Gospels give us the teaching of Jesus,

and the rest of the New Testament, including 2 Thessalonians 2, is the further explanation of that teaching by those who knew Jesus."

There is no one right way to do what I am suggesting, but as you can see from the example above, I always try to do three things. First, I try to connect what my students are about to read to the whole layout of the New Testament. Second, I try to connect what they are about to read to the teaching of Jesus and His mission. Third, I try to show them specifically how the texts in the New Testament connect (e.g., how 2 Thessalonians connects to Acts 17 and Matthew 24). This is, admittedly, easier to do in some places in the New Testament than others, but this is what students need to have proper context for what they read and to adequately understand the story and message of the New Testament.

The Story and Message of the New Testament

The task of teaching the story and message of the New Testament to students does not have to be a tremendously difficult exercise. Simple summaries can be accurate without being comprehensive. I do not have to say everything there is to say about the story and message of the New Testament, but I do need to give them an adequate summary to help them place the text that we are studying into its larger context. Here are some sample summaries that I have found helpful to give to my students:

The Gospels – The Gospels record the birth, ministry, death, and resurrection of Jesus. Each of the four Gospels was written by a different person to a different audience, so each Gospel focuses on different aspects of the Jesus story. All of the Gospels present Jesus as God who came to earth in the person of Jesus as the fulfillment of the Old Testament promises of a savior. God saves us from our sins by sending Jesus to die in our place, as the sufficient substitute for our sins. Jesus then rose again from the dead and offers forgiveness and eternal life to all who believe in Him. Jesus, Himself, in the

Gospels, teaches us about the kingdom of God and God's salvation through miracles and in sermons and parables, using the Old Testament as His Bible.

Acts – The book of Acts picks up right where the Gospels end. Jesus commanded His disciples to take the good news of the gospel of Jesus to the ends of the earth, and then Jesus ascended into Heaven.

The first half of the book of Acts tells the story of the gospel in Jerusalem and the surrounding regions. The Apostle Peter is the focal character. The second half of the book of Acts focuses on the Apostle Paul and tells the story of the gospel going to the ends of the earth as Paul traveled the Mediterranean world in order to get the gospel to places it has never been. The book of Acts ends with Paul's arrest and imprisonment in Rome. The book makes clear, however, that Jesus' global mission is still going strong under the efforts of Paul from his prison cell in Rome. The book is written to us so all Christians (including us) will understand their mission is our mission as well.

Paul's Epistles – The story and message of Paul's letters are best understood when read in the "Acts order" (chronologically).[4] Paul's letters divide into three groups, representing the three phases of his ministry.

Galatians, 1 & 2 Thessalonians, 1 & 2 Corinthians, and Romans are Paul's missionary letters. They were written to groups of Christians he had visited or planned to visit during his missionary travels. Each of Paul's missionary journeys took him farther and farther from the Middle East. Paul traveled to Turkey (Galatia) and Greece (Thessalonica and Corinth), and he planned to go to Italy (Rome). In these letters, Paul communicated the gospel and the teaching of Jesus primarily to non-Jews, most of whom were brand-new Chris-

---

[4] Scholars typically understand there to be four phases to Paul's ministry. The pre-mission phase (Acts 7–9); the missionary journeys (Acts 13–20); Paul's arrest, trials, and imprisonment in Rome (Acts 21–28); and Paul's subsequent release and attempted fourth missionary Journey to Spain. These events most likely take place after the events of Acts 28.

tians. Paul explained and defended the gospel in his letters as well as answered questions about the teaching of Jesus. Paul also explained, in detail, how Jesus-followers ought to live out the gospel in their day-to-day lives and dealt with problems in the churches related to Christian living. These letters, like all of Paul's letters, were also written with a wider readership and with later audiences in mind.[5]

Ephesians, Philippians, Colossians, and Philemon are Paul's prison letters. Near the end of the book of Acts, Paul was arrested and ultimately imprisoned in Rome. During his imprisonment, he wrote four more letters to places he has been already as a missionary (Ephesus and Philippi), to places he wanted to go but couldn't because he was in prison (Colossae), and to a person in need of Christian teaching (Philemon). In these letters, Paul expanded upon what he has already explained in his earlier letters, and he offered new insights into the teaching of Jesus.

First & Second Timothy and Titus are the Pastoral Letters. They were written near the end of Paul's life after the events of the book of Acts. Paul was preparing a mission trip to Spain and wanted to leave the churches in the eastern Mediterranean with plenty of support. So, Paul placed his two top disciples, Timothy and Titus, in two geographically key locations, Ephesus and Crete. As Paul prepared for his trip to Spain, he wrote each of these men a letter (1 Timothy and Titus). These letters are called the Pastoral Letters because they focus on things that concern church leaders (qualification for elders and deacons, how discipleship happens in a church, how to do benevolence, how to minister to people who don't want to listen, etc.). Then Paul headed toward Spain. Scholars do not know how far he made it before he was rearrested and back in prison in Rome, but

---

[5] There are many clear indications throughout Paul's letters that he was writing with other, later audiences in mind. In 1 Corinthians 5 and 8, rather than simply answer the questions raised by the Corinthians (which he did in just a few sentences), Paul went to great pains to explain in detail how to think Christianly about these issues. Paul anticipated other readers and other situations in which these teachings might be applied. In Colossians 4, Paul instructed the church to read earlier letters he wrote to someone else and to be sure the letter they have from him gets to othr Christians as well.

that is where he was when he wrote 2 Timothy.[6] This book serves as the last testimony of Paul to his disciples before his death. In it, Paul reminds us all to remain faithful to Christ no matter the difficulty and even when no one else is faithful.

The heart of Paul's theological teaching in all his letters is this: Jesus is the Savior, and He offers us salvation by faith, as a work of God, and not as a result of our own works. The heart of Paul's ethical teaching and all of Christian living is this: meditate on what God has for done for you in Christ and then behave that way toward other people. This is what Paul calls the "law of Christ." Paul teaches us how to think about the gospel, how to think about the Old Testament, and how to live out the gospel in a way that is consistent with the teaching of Jesus as we live out the Great Commission.

General Letters – The General Letters were written over a wide span of time and to a varied audience. The authors of the General Letters—apostles and others who were closely associated with Jesus or His apostles[7]—explain the teaching of Jesus and encourage Christian living. Like many of Paul's letters, the General Letters were written to specific circumstances and answer specific questions or deal with particular problems. Also, like Paul's letters, these letters were written with a wider readership and later audiences in mind.

Though they have very different stories, the messages of the general letters are amazingly cohesive and relevant. The book of Hebrews is written to Jewish Christians, probably in Rome, who are in danger of abandoning Christian practice to avoid persecution. The author wrote to remind them and us that Jesus is better than anything, even avoiding persecution, and he called all Christians to remain faithful during their hardships. James wrote to a Jewish

---

[6] There are a variety of theories as to how many times Paul was in prison. The "two-imprisonment" theory is historically the most popular. There are some early Christian traditions that suggest Paul may have made it to Spain before his rearrest and subsequent execution.

[7] A good case can be made that all the authors of the general letters were people who actually knew Jesus when He was on earth. Peter and John were Jesus' disciples, and there is tradition and textual evidence to suggest that James and Jude were Jesus' earthly brothers, the sons of Mary and Joseph. These two were also very closely associated with the Apostles in Jerusalem.

Christian congregation outside of Jerusalem. His five-part exhortation reads like a sermon to encourage all Christians everywhere to continue on to maturity in the faith. Peter wrote two letters to Christians living in Asia Minor to help them to think Christianly about persecution and suffering and to prepare them for the inevitable coming of false teachers to their doorsteps. First Peter stands today as the most comprehensive discussion of suffering in the New Testament, and both Jude and 2 Peter's descriptions of false teachers sound like they were ripped from today's news headlines. John wrote three letters to congregations in and around Ephesus after a huge blow-up with a group of false teachers. John encouraged the churches that they have believed in the right Jesus and the fact that the false teachers departed is not a failure on the part of the faithful. John also wrote practical advice about how to encourage the work of the global mission and to make sure it continues because the world is, then and now, filled with false teachers.

Revelation – The New Testament ends with a promise, a promise that God is going to finish what He started. God is going to fix the world that we broke with our sin, and He is going to do it with both grace and judgment. To communicate this promise God gave the Apostle John a series of visions that he then crafted into an Old-Testament-style literary apocalypse. The wild imagery, which has its origins in the Old Testament, shows them and us that though the world is going to get worse for a time, God has not forgotten His promise. He will rescue those in the Lamb's book of life, and He will judge the world. Powerful people will try to stop Him, and Satan himself will try to stop Him, but God will not be thwarted. He will usher in the return of His Son as the righteous King and remake and restore the whole world. Revelation is a crazy ride, but it is also a powerful encouragement to all those who follow Jesus to remain faithful, regardless of how crazy the world gets. God knows what He is doing, and it will all end just as He has planned.

The New Testament is an anthology, a collection of the writings and teachings of the people who knew Jesus best. That does not mean it is not also a book that tells one story, the story of the gospel. The Gospels—Matthew, Mark, Luke, and John—record the teachings of Jesus about the gospel, the good news of God's salvation in Christ. Acts shows the church of Jesus taking that good news to the ends of the earth. The letters—Paul's and others—explain the teaching of Jesus and His gospel to followers of Jesus then and now. And the book of Revelation explains the culmination of the gospel at the end of the age.

CHAPTER 4

LEARNING FROM OUR ANCIENT TEXT THROUGH THE AGES

Peter Beck, Ph.D.

"Take it and read, take it and read." – Augustine, Confessions, VIII:12

Sung by a child nearby, Augustine (354–430) took these words as a sign. He sprung to his feet, ran across his yard, and retrieved the Bible he had recently flung aside in frustration. Opening to Romans 13:13-14, Augustine heard God spoke to him directly. There the apostle Paul wrote, "Let us walk properly as in the daytime, not in orgies and drunkenness, not in sexual immorality and sensuality, not in quarreling and jealousy. But put on the Lord Jesus Christ, and make no provision for the flesh, to gratify its desires" (ESV). Seeing his sin through the eyes of God, convinced this text spoke to his sinful proclivities, Augustine surrendered his life to the Lord. As he later confessed, "For in an instant, as I came to the end of that sentence, it was as though the light of confidence flooded into my heart and all the darkness of doubt was dispelled."[1]

Augustine's newfound view of Scripture reflected that of the early church. The words of the prophets and the apostles were held inviolate and understood to be the *regula fidei*, the rule of faith which governed Christian life and thought. That was not always the case. Theological troublemakers like Marcion (85–160), who excised portions of the New Testament he believed were too Jewish, and Arius (250/256–336), who denied the deity of Christ, arose periodically to challenge the church's convictions about Scripture. Each time the church ultimately returned to the Bible to correct its course.

The same course correction is needed today. Sixteen hundred years after Augustine's conversion, many who claim the name of Christ express contradictory views of the Bible. One survey found nearly 92% of Protestant teenagers professed a high view of Scripture.[2] Another survey, however, revealed less than one-half (47%) of Christian teenagers from around the world believe Jesus was crucified. Just one-third confess He was raised from the dead.[3] Clearly, it's time for the church to do a better job of discipling her young and offering them a defense of the Bible's accuracy and authority.

Church history is a great place to turn for these lessons. A short survey of key turning points in the history of the church follows. These turning points came when the church turned back to the Bible.

Controversies, Creeds, and Canon

"These [books] are the fountains of salvation, that they who thirst may be satisfied with the living words they contain." – Athanasius, Easter Letter (367)

---

[1] Augustine, *Confessions*, VIII:12.
[2] Barna. *Top 10 Findings on Teens and the Bible*. 2016. Retrieved from https://www.barna.com/research/top-10-findings-teens-bible/.
[3] Barna. *A Sneak Peek into Barna's Global Study of Teens*. 11 May, 2022, Retrieved from https://www.barna.com/research/introducing-open-generation/.

Shortly after the birth of the church, the apostles and their disciples began writing books and letters affirming the Gospel and explaining its implications. Churches held onto these writings and shared them with one another. Over time this body of literature grew along with the church. With growth came new challenges. For the early church, the greatest challenges were persecution and confusion.

In the first 250 years, Christians faced ten periods of persecution. Beginning with Nero, whose violence against the church took the lives of Paul and Peter, Roman persecution came and went with the mood of the prevailing emperor. Most of these seasons of tribulation were short-lived and narrow in scope. Three, however, consumed Christians across the empire. The worst and last took place under the emperor Diocletian (r. 284–305). At his behest, churches were burned, pastors executed, and Bibles destroyed. Providentially, this ended with his demise in the year 305. With the rise of his eventual successor, Constantine, the church entered a period of political tranquility and theological controversy.

Constantine's "Edict of Milan" (313) granted the church legal protections enjoyed by a host of other religions across the empire. With newfound peace, Christians could once again promote and explore their faith. Free of the fear of arrest, Christian theologians began to debate the great truths at the heart of orthodox thinking. Ironically, one such debate so threatened the political peace the emperor demanded a resolution.

At liberty to study the Bible freely, Arius shared his theological conclusions with students in Alexandria, Egypt. His thoughts alarmed the bishop, Alexander, who banished him from the region. What was so dangerous about Arius' beliefs? He denied the eternality and deity of Jesus. Citing some biblical texts (e.g., John 14:28) while ignoring others, Arius infamously claimed, "there was a time when the Son was not." According to Arius, Jesus was the first and greatest of all God's creation who then created everything else. Exiled, Arius fled to the east where another bishop offered him protection and a platform from which he could continue to share his unorthodox views.

Unable to sit idly by, Alexander sought to put an end to it. This began a series of events that threatened to destabilize the peace. Constantine called for a council to resolve the issue. This council met in the ancient city of Nicaea, in what is now northwestern Turkey, in 325. Approximately 300 bishops gathered there, heard the charges, and listened intently to the theological debate that followed. Alexander's protégé, Athanasius, provided a compelling case for the deity of Christ from Scripture. Following his lead, the council produced a statement, the Nicene Creed, outlining its biblical convictions affirming Jesus' deity. With the Nicene Creed the church averted a theological crisis and explained an orthodox Christology still maintained today.

With the focus on theological nuance and precision, the role of the Bible in this debate often remains underappreciated. Arius and Athanasius both sought to ground their views in Scripture. What made this possible, and the Council necessary, was the growing availability of Scripture and the freedom to read it. The question that begged to be asked was, "What constitutes the Bible?" No single event or person can claim to be the final word on the closing of the canon of Scripture. The process took place over time. However, by the time the bishops had gathered in Nicaea, that debate was closed. The books were set. Athanasius himself affirmed all twenty-seven books of the New Testament in his "Easter Letter" of 367. It was his conviction that all of Scripture bore testimony to Jesus' deity that drove him to stand up to Arius. As he later wrote, these books were "divinely inspired." "In these alone is proclaimed the doctrine of godliness."[4] Thus, Athanasius turned to Scripture alone to defeat Arianism and defend orthodoxy.

---

[4] Athanasius, "Easter Letter" (367).

Renaissance, Reformation, and a Return to the Bible

"Here I stand. I can do no other. God help me. Amen." – Martin Luther, Diet of Worms (1521)

As the Middle Ages gave way to the Renaissance, the church found itself in trouble again. The Eastern and Western branches of the church excommunicated one another in 1054. Islam had since conquered much of the East. The West struggled to adapt to changing times and to solve its own problems. Despite repeated efforts to right its course, the Western Church suffered from theological and ethical malaise that threatened its existence.

Whereas Scholasticism and Conciliar Reform failed to fix the acknowledged problems in the church, universities unwittingly offered a solution. The Renaissance brought about a rebirth of learning. With its emphasis on human value and ability, Renaissance thought called scholars to *ad fontes*—to come back to the fount or source. Armed with this mantra, theologians returned to Scripture unencumbered by layers of tradition and interpretation. As Erasmus (1466–1536) said in his newly translated Greek edition of the New Testament, "I perceived that that teaching which is our salvation was to be had in a much purer and more lively form if sought at the fountain-head and drawn from the actual sources than from pools and runnels."[5] Unintentionally, committed Catholics like Erasmus provided the resources for the coming Reformation.

History remembers Martin Luther (1483–1546) as the author of the "95 Theses" and the protagonist of the Protestant Reformation. Luther's contributions, both theological and political, prove difficult to number. Attempting to pinpoint his greatest gift to the church, theologians often point to his rediscovery of the doctrine of justification by faith alone. Responding to Erasmus, Luther claimed his work on the bondage of the will to be one of the two most important works he produced. This doctrine, he claimed, was

---

[5] Desiderius Erasmus, "Author's Dedication," *Novum Instrumentum*.

the point of disagreement between the Protestants and the Roman Catholic Church.[6]

When pushed to renounce his theological convictions, however, Martin Luther revealed his primary motivation. With his life potentially on the line, Luther refused to recant and appealed to the Bible: "Unless I shall be convinced by the testimonies of the Scriptures or by clear reason.... I neither can nor will make any retraction, since it is neither safe nor honorable to act against conscience." Having made his stand, Luther returned home. Along the way, however, allies staged a "kidnapping" to save the Reformer's life from the Pope's condemnation.

"Exiled" in Wartburg Castle, Luther began what might have been his greatest contribution to the church—a translation of the Bible into the language of the common man. John Wycliffe had tried to do so 140 years earlier in England. His efforts landed him in jail where he died before his persecutors could execute him. Safely sequestered in the castle, Luther produced a German translation of the New Testament in just 10 weeks. Thanks to his efforts and Gutenberg's printing press, invented just decades earlier, Luther unleashed a wave of Bible translations that has not subsided yet. As of 2020, Christians can access the complete Bible in over 700 languages and the New Testament in over 1500 more.

Movements, Missions, and the Message

"The Holy Scripture is the only sufficient, certain, and infallible rule of all saving knowledge, faith, and obedience." – Second London Confession of Faith (1689).

Early Protestants produced many confessions of faith, explaining their beliefs, defending their positions, and delineating their differences. Ultimately, they desired to express their agreement with the historic faith of the Church. Regardless of differences on ecclesial

---

[6] Martin Luther, *Bondage of the Will* (London: James Clark, 1957), 31.

matters, the early Protestants were committed to "the faith once for all handed down to the saints" (Jude 3). The earliest confessions followed the outlines of early creedal statements by beginning with the doctrine of God. In the 1600s, believers in England broke with this tradition. The Westminster Confession of Faith (1647) opened with a statement on Scripture. Baptists appropriated this belief statement and made it their own by beginning with a statement about the Bible's primacy and efficacy.

The next century saw a wave of religious and social activism sweep across England. William Wilberforce (1759–1833) launched the Society for the Prevention of Cruelty to Animals and fought tirelessly to bring about the end of the slave trade. Others began societies to promote manners and temperance. William Carey (1761–1834) decided to change the world.

The cobbler-turned-pastor became concerned about the plight of the unreached peoples of the world through his readings about Captain Cook's travels. Moved by the tales of spiritual darkness and convicted by Scripture that it was incumbent upon all believers to share the gospel, Carey convinced his fellow Baptist ministers to form the Baptist Missionary Society in 1792. Carey was more than an organizer; he was a missionary. When the group asked about the next steps for their new enterprise, they asked, "Who will go?" Carey volunteered, "I will go down [to India] but remember that you must hold the ropes." With that bold statement, the Modern Missions Movement, with its new way of funding missionary efforts, began.

The story of Carey's move to India in 1793 and the struggles he faced is heroic and spiritually encouraging. The work accomplished was staggering. The emphasis on the Bible should challenge Christians today.

Carey, along with his eventual teammates, John Marshman and William Ward, settled into the work in India. To accomplish their mission, the three exercised a three-fold approach to their ministry based on their individual talents. Marshman preached the Word to the indigenous population. Carey translated it into the native languages. Ward printed it for those they taught to read. In addition to untold numbers led to the faith by their efforts during their lifetimes, millions more would be impacted by their labor of love in the years to come.

Though largely uneducated, the self-taught Carey proved to be quite the linguist. As a young pastor, Carey learned to read Greek, Hebrew, Latin, Dutch, and French on his own. Once firmly established in India, Carey learned and taught Hindi and Sanskrit to English bureaucrats when they arrived in the country. He translated ancient Indian texts back into Hindi from the languages of their conquerors. Before he died, William Carey translated the Bible into nearly 40 languages. What drove Carey? "I have God," he wrote, "and his word is sure; ... my hope, fixed on that sure word, will rise superior to all expectations."[7] Having never returned to England, William Carey lived and died trying to make sure others shared that hope. Today, in no small part due to the efforts of Carey and others like him, there are nearly 30 million Christians in India, a number that is expected to rise to 50 million by 2050.

Rejection, Revolution, and Revelation

"The New Testament canon was formed by the 'winners' of the theological battles within early Christianity and therefore is filled with their preferred books." – F.C. Baur

Ironically, even as Carey and company were taking the Word to the unreached peoples of the East, Christians in the West were questioning the very validity of that Word. The Enlightenment opened an age of biblical skepticism. For some, the quest for the historical Jesus, not the one presented in the Bible, was on. Scholars like Hermann Reimarus (1694–1768) denied the historicity of

---

[7] William Carey, *Periodical Accounts Relative to the Baptist Missionary Society* (London: W. Button, 1810), 1:175.

the miracles. Friedrich Schleiermacher (1768–1834), the Father of Modern Liberalism, praised Jesus for His God awareness instead of His deity. Old Testament scholar Julius Wellhausen (1844–1918) questioned the Mosaic authorship of the Pentateuch. By the early 20th century, for men like Harry Emerson Fosdick (1878–1969), there was no shame in publicly questioning long-held orthodoxy on positions like the Virgin Birth, the bodily resurrection of Christ, or His physical return. For many, it seemed, the battle for the Bible was over.

While many Christians fell prey to the alluring thoughts of modernism and liberalism, not all abdicated the faith. Defenders of the faith rose up across the Western world. In England, Charles Spurgeon (1834–1892) fought to forestall the downgrade he saw among those in the Baptist Union. In the United States, entire denominations rose or fell over the issue of Scripture's authority and truthfulness. Among the Presbyterians, J. Gresham Machen (1881–1937) and his colleagues at Princeton refused to stand idly by. Forming their own missionary agency and then their own seminary, the sought to return their denomination to the faith of Westminster.

In the midst of the Princeton Controversy, Machen masterfully defined the struggle in 1922. "The great redemptive religion which has always been known as Christianity is battling against a totally different type of religious belief, which is only the more destructive of the Christian faith because it makes use of traditional Christian terminology," he argued.[8] Their religion, Machen concluded, was not Christianity at all.[9] Why? Individual experience replaced biblical authority, eventually dethroning even Jesus who ascribed such authority to Scripture that was then jettisoned in favor of personal opinion. As Machen summarized so clearly 100 years ago,

---

[8] J. Gresham Machen, *Christianity and Liberalism* (Grand Rapids: Eerdmans, 1999), 2.
[9] Machen, 8.

> It is no wonder, then that liberalism is totally different from Christianity, for the foundation is different. Christianity is founded upon the Bible. It bases upon the Bible both its thinking and its life. Liberalism on the other hand is founded upon the shifting emotions of sinful men.[10]

In the intervening years, the battle has not abated. Some denominations surrendered the high ground and joined the ranks of those who questioned the inspiration and authority of Scripture. Others were created as safe havens for those who wished to hold fast to the mystery long ago revealed by God. A select few fought back and returned their churches to the orthodox fold. But not all.

Conclusion

As the Teacher once said, "There is nothing new under the sun" (Ecclesiastes 1:9, ESV). Thus, the modern church finds itself in the throes of battles fought long ago for the same reason. Once more another generation of Christ followers are ignorant of or ignore the very Ancient Text that tells them of the Christ they claim to love. That text, the Bible, still speaks to every debate and wind of controversy that blows, if only we would turn back to it. Read it. Teach it. Live it. After all, as Paul wrote 2000 years ago, God inspired the biblical authors so "that the man of God may be complete, equipped for every good work" (2 Timothy 3:16-17, ESV). Let's learn the lessons of the past before it's too late. Let's trust God's Word to lead us into the future.

[10] Machen, 79.

CHAPTER 5

TRUSTING AND APPLYING OUR ANCIENT TEXT

Jonathan D. Watson, Ph.D.

"Do you believe in gravity?" No one's ever asked me this question. (I suspect your experience matches mine.) However, I can imagine that if you or I were asked this question, it would be a bit disorienting. Why? Because in our society gravity is a basic presupposition, a belief that we have held since childhood. As such, we've never had to defend the concept, we've simply taken the reality and truthfulness of gravity for granted. This is sometimes the case for Christian students (especially those raised in a Christian home) as it relates to any number of foundational Christian teachings, including the nature of the Bible itself. The reliability and trustworthiness of the Christian Scriptures have often been taken for granted within the church. The modern world, however, rejects this basic belief.

"Do you trust your Bible? Do you believe it is true and trustworthy? Are the words of Scripture 'God's words'? Does the Bible carry God's authority?" Faithful Christians across history would answer each of these questions with a resounding "Yes!" However, students today are regularly confronted with objections and counterclaims to this foundational Christian belief. On what basis can one have the confidence to trust that the Scriptures are in fact God's Word and are trustworthy for teaching us who God is, the purpose of life, where the world has gone wrong, and how we can be made right with Him and with one another? This chapter will provide a theological foundation and framework for such confidence. It will not address every objection. There will be much left unsaid. However, our purpose here will be to develop an outline for answering the question, "Can we trust the ancient text of the Bible?" The goal is to provide theological foundation stones for confidence in God's Word upon which students and student leaders can continue to build.

Before we begin considering the biblical text directly, we need to see how the Scriptures fit into the larger doctrine of God. This is important because understanding who God is will make all the difference in how we think about the Scriptures as God's Word and what that means for our lives.

Does God Speak? The God Who Eternally Speaks (God's Triunity)

The doctrine of the Trinity is significant for understanding the Scriptures as *God's Word*.[1] Why? Because the Scriptures aren't the first time God has spoken. God has eternally been *speaking* or communicating in love from Father to Son and Spirit. We see this throughout the life of Jesus. Jesus, the eternal Son of God, speaks to His Father (e.g., Matthew 11:25; Luke 23:46), communicates the words of His Father (John 14:10; 17:14), and, in turn, the Father speaks of and is well-pleased with the Son (Matthew 3:17; 17:5; cf. Mark 1:11; 9:7; Luke 3:22; 2 Peter 1:17).[2] In this way, the Triune

---

[1] We can define the doctrine in three statements: 1) There is one God, 2) this God eternally exists in three persons: Father, Son, and Holy Spirit, and 3) each person is fully God. Evangelicals have often neglected the doctrine of the Trinity and under-appreciated its significance. For accessible treatments see Michael Reeves, *Delighting in the Trinity: An Introduction to the Christian Faith* (IVP Academic, 2012); Scott Swain, *The Trinity: An Introduction*, Short Studies in Systematic Theology (Crossway, 2020). Reeves is my recommended starting point.

[2] Note that Jesus didn't just become the Son in His incarnation; He's eternally been the Son. For an accessible and engaging exploration of the doctrine of the incarnation that resonates well with teens see Todd Miles, *Superheroes Can't Save You: Epic Examples of Historic*

God is a communicating God through and through. Thus, the Scriptures are an overflowing extension of the eternally Triune God who has eternally been in conversation with Himself. He is a God brimming with words.

What Happens When God Speaks?

If the eternal, Triune God is a God who communicates, so what? What happens when God speaks? How weighty, significant, and durable are His words? To answer these questions, we may briefly look at two issues: 1) Creation and 2) Salvation.

Creation

First, God speaks in creation. When God began to create (out of His free grace and over-flowing love and generosity[3]) He *spoke* it into existence. He created with His word: "And God said, 'Let there be light,' and there was light" (Genesis 1:3, ESV).[4] Looking back at creation, the psalmist writes, "For he spoke, and it came to be; he commanded, and it stood firm" (Psalm 33:9, ESV). This word-centered act of creation is a manifestation of who God is. Graeme Goldsworthy writes,

> It may seem to be stating the obvious to say that God is a speaking God. He created all things by a word. Why a word? Why not a thought or a (metaphorical) snap of the fingers? We can say with certainty that he chose both to create and to communicate with his creation by his spoken word. If there is a discernible

---

Heresies (Nashville: B&H Academic, 2018). Miles helps us see how the full divinity and full humanity of Jesus matters for our salvation.

[3] See Kelly Kapic, *The God Who Gives: How the Trinity Shapes the Christian Story*, rev. ed. of *God So Loved He Gave* (Zondervan, 2018), 21. See also Reeves, *Delighting in the Trinity*, 31 and Chapter 2 (esp. 57, 61–62).

[4] For helpful commentary notes on the text, I recommend the *ESV Study Bible* (Wheaton, IL: Crossway, 2008).

> reason for this word-centered activity of God, it lies in the fact that it is his attribute to be a speaking God.[5]

Thus, God's act of speaking creation into existence reveals to us both that God is a God who communicates and that when He speaks His words have powerful, lasting effect. All of creation bears witness to God's declaration about His Word: "it shall not return to me empty, but it shall accomplish that which I purpose, and it shall succeed in the thing for which I sent it" (Isaiah 55:11b, ESV).

The effectiveness of God's Word is matched by its durability: God's Word doesn't have an expiration date. Psalm 119 is the richest reflection upon the goodness of God's Word in the entire Bible. There we read "Forever, O LORD, your word is firmly fixed in the heavens" (Psalm 119:89), "The sum of your word is truth, and every one of your righteous rules endures forever" (Psalm 119:160, ESV). Isaiah writes, "The grass withers, the flower fades, but the word of our God will stand forever" (Isaiah 40:8, ESV; cf. 1 Peter 1:22–25). God's Word is "firmly fixed," it "endures" and "stands forever." In short, God's Word is eternal.

Salvation

Second, God speaks in salvation. God created the world and humankind by His word. He also placed Adam and Eve in the Garden of Eden and gave them a word to live by (Genesis 2:17). Unfortunately, Adam and Eve decided to disbelieve God's Word and instead trusted the word of the serpent (Genesis 3:1–7). When God confronts Adam and Eve about their sin, He not only addresses their sin with judgment, but He simultaneously gives to them a word of promise. He promises to send a Rescuer through the line of Eve who will defeat Satan, sin, and death (Genesis 3:15). As the biblical story moves forward, God continues to speak words of judgment and hope. He makes covenants (promises or agreements) with Noah, Abraham, Isaac, Jacob, Moses, and David. The *big take away* for our purposes

---

[5] Graeme Goldsworthy, "A Biblical-Theological Perspective on Prayer," *The Southern Baptist Journal of Theology*, 10, no. 4 (2006): 15.

is to see that salvation history is characterized by God speaking to His people, reiterating and clarifying the details of the salvation He is working. These covenants are expressions of God's steadfast, covenantal love for His people, and God repeatedly emphasizes the fact that He will not fail to make good on His promises (even though His people have and will repeatedly prove unfaithful).[6]

The "good news" declared in the New Testament is that these covenant promises find their fulfillment in Jesus Christ of Nazareth, God's Son and our Savior (Mark 1:15; 2 Corinthians 1:20). As the author of Hebrews puts it, "Long ago, at many times and in many ways, God spoke to our fathers by the prophets, but in these last days he has spoken to us by his Son, whom he appointed the heir of all things, through whom also he created the world" (Hebrews 1:1-2). Jesus is the full and final revelation of God to humanity. The Apostle John describes Jesus as "the Word" (John 1:1) and Jesus declares in his High Priestly prayer, "For I have given them the words that you gave me, and they have received them and have come to know in truth that I came from you; and they have believed that you sent me" (John 17:8). As we saw with God's word in creation, these words of truth that save and sanctify are effective and endure forever. Peter, quoting the prophet Isaiah writes, "'The grass withers, and the flower falls, but the word of the Lord remains forever.' And this word is the good news that was preached to you" (1 Peter 1:24b-25).

In summary, the Triune God is a God who speaks. His speaking preceded creation and salvation, but creation and salvation are the products of His speech. When God speaks, whatever He intends to happen, happens. His words will not fall to the ground without ef-

---

[6] Psalm 136 takes the reader through God's mighty acts of creation (verses 4–9), salvation through the Exodus (verses 10–15) and wilderness wanderings and conquest of the land (verses 16–22), to the present day of the psalmist (perhaps after the return from exile?; verses 23–25). At each turning point, the psalmist pauses to reflect upon the fact that God's "steadfast love endures forever." Importantly, this steadfast love is expressed definitively in the many covenants God has made with His people.

fect; they are eternal. These fundamental truths are incredibly important to the trustworthiness of Scripture.

Is the Bible God's Word and Can We Trust What God Says?

In 2 Timothy 3:16, the apostle Paul states that "All Scripture (*graphē*) is breathed out by God (*theopneustos*)" The term *theopneustos* literally means *God-breathed* and points us to the divine source of the Scriptures. In saying this Paul affirms that everything rightly called "Scripture" (the "sacred writings" as referenced in 2 Timothy 3:15) finds its source in God. Similarly, Peter's second letter (2 Peter 1:21) affirms that the process of inspiration was accomplished by God the Holy Spirit. This further clarifies the apostles' understanding of how God produced Scripture through human authors: He did so through the work of His Holy Spirit.

When we ask the question "Is the Bible God's Word?" we are asking the question of source. The Christian doctrine of inspiration answers this question, and its answer shapes our understanding of the Scriptures in at least three significant ways: authority, character, and interpretation.

Authority

First, the source of the Scriptures determines the level of authority we recognize in the text. For example, I have four children. On occasion, I will ask one of them to go into the backyard to call a sibling in for dinner. The child—let's say it's one of my daughters—is happy to fulfill this request. However, she very well may go into the backyard and bossily declare: "Come inside!" If this were to happen, how do you imagine her sibling will respond? If you guessed that the sibling would blow her off, you are correct! Why? Because she is simply telling her sibling what to do on her own authority. If, however, she says, "Daddy (or Mommy) said it was time to come in for dinner" the sibling (in theory) would respond much differently. Why? Because my daughter is no longer speaking on her own authority, but rather, she is reporting the words of a parent. While she isn't the parent, she has Daddy's word, and that word carries Daddy's authority. Do you see the connection to inspiration? Inspiration is all about the source of the Scriptures. If these words are sourced in God, then they carry God's authority. This affects how we read and respond to the text of Scripture.

Character

A second area of importance, related to the first, is the character of the Scripture. If the Scriptures are sourced in God, then we are right to expect that they reflect God's character. Prominent among the many attributes of God spoken of in the Scriptures is that of truthfulness: God doesn't lie. For example, we read that God's "words are true" (2 Samuel 7:28), "God is not man, that he should lie" (Numbers 23:19), "every word of God proves true" (Proverbs 30:5), God "never lies" (Titus 1:2), and, in fact, "It is impossible for God to lie" (Hebrews 6:18).[7] God's holiness and righteousness are reflected by His word. "The words of the LORD are pure words, like silver refined in a furnace on the ground, purified seven times" (Psalm 12:6, ESV). Jesus put it simply in His High Priestly prayer to the Father, "Sanctify them in the truth; your word is truth" (John 17:17, ESV). An affirmation of inspiration, that the Scriptures are sourced in God, brings with it the affirmation that they bear God's character and are truthful on everything to which they speak.[8]

---

[7] There are three great psalms that reflect upon the goodness of God's Word (Torah/Law/Instruction): Psalm 1, 19, and 119. It is a fruitful exercise to read these Psalms in one sitting. Psalm 119 is an acrostic poem organized around the Hebrew alphabet. There are 22 stanzas each with 8 lines. As 22 is divisible by 7 with 1 remainder, I have found it a helpful practice (from time to time) to read 3 stanzas each day of the week as a prelude to my normal Bible reading (I read the extra stanza on Saturday). This has provided a wonderful reminder to me of the goodness and trustworthiness of God's Word before I read from wherever I might be scheduled to read in my Bible reading plan.

[8] The twin doctrines of biblical infallibility and inerrancy mentioned in Dr. Jackson's chapter on biblical authority are directly connected to our affirmation here. The most important statement on biblical inerrancy is the "Chicago Statement on Biblical Inerrancy" (1978). An electronic copy of this statement is available from https://www.etsjets.org/files/documents/Chicago_Statement.pdf. This statement lays out in both positive and negative affirmations on what the doctrine of inerrancy means and does not mean. For a helpful collection of essays that explain and defend the doctrine see John MacArthur, ed. *The Inerrant Word: Biblical, Historical, Theological, and Pastoral Perspectives* (Wheaton: Crossway, 2016).

Interpretation

Finally, the doctrine of inspiration is important on the level of interpretation. The biblical canon is comprised of 66 books. While some of those books have been penned by the same person (e.g., John, Luke, Peter, or Paul), there are a wide number of authors represented. If the source of these books is simply each of these authors, then we should expect no agreement between them. But if the source of these books is singular (i.e., God), then we should expect there to be a unity to their contents and message. Thus, when apparent disagreement emerges (e.g., Paul's teaching that one is justified by faith apart from works and James' teaching that faith without works is dead) we are prompted to consider more carefully how these authors may be understood to agree.

In sum, if the Scriptures are sourced in God, then they are 1) supremely authoritative (no other authority is higher), 2) truthful in all that they teach (bearing God's holy, righteous character), and 3) unified (i.e., truth is non-contradictory).

An Authoritative and Trustworthy Text: Old and New Testament as Scripture?

To this point, I've tried to show that 1) God is a God who speaks, 2) God's Word is powerful and accomplishes its intended effect, 3) God's Word is eternal, 4) God's Word bears His character and is therefore trustworthy and true, and 5) the Scriptures are God's Word. In this final section I want to spend a little more time to help us see how and why both the Old Testament (OT) and New Testament (NT) are rightly included in the category of holy, *God-breathed Scripture*.

Taking Our Cues From Jesus

Jesus' view of the OT Scriptures is the starting place for the church's understanding of the Bible. As we will see, Jesus also sets the stage for us to expect further revelation through His apostles. If someone has accepted the testimony that Jesus Christ is God's Son who has become our Savior through His incarnation, substitutionary death, burial, and resurrection, then His claims and His teaching are the starting point for our view of everything.

Several key themes are evident in Jesus' view of the Scriptures. First, Jesus saw the OT Scriptures as the Word of God that "cannot be broken" (John 10:35). Indeed, "until heaven and earth pass away, not an iota, not a dot,[9] will pass from the Law until all is accomplished" (Matthew 5:18, ESV). His purpose was not to abolish the Law of Moses but to fulfill it (Matthew 5:17). This theme aligns with the understanding of God's Word developed earlier: when God speaks, His word powerfully and without fail accomplishes what it is intended to accomplish. His word lasts forever. Its authority cannot be trumped. Its purposes cannot fail.

Second, Jesus saw the OT Scriptures as a key witness to who He was and what He had come to do.[10] We are told that on the day that He rose from the dead He appeared to two disciples on the road to Emmaus and rebuked them for their slowness to believe the reports of His resurrection, asking "Was it not necessary that the Christ should suffer these things and enter into his glory?" (Luke 24:26, ESV). Importantly, to address their error we are told that "beginning with Moses and all the Prophets, he interpreted to them in all the Scriptures the things concerning himself" (Luke 24:27, ESV). Jesus later appeared to His other disciples and used the OT Scriptures to help them see that everything that had happened in His

---

[9] These are the smallest characters and strokes in the alphabet.

[10] Jesus' own works and even the divine voice of the Father from Heaven also bore witness about His divine identity as well (see John 5, esp. verses 30–37; Matthew 3:17; 17:5).

crucifixion, burial, and resurrection had been predicted there (Luke 24:44–49).[11]

Third, Jesus quoted the OT as authoritative for godly living. When tempted by the devil in the wilderness, Jesus responded each time by quoting Scripture ("It is written"; Matthew 4:4, 7, 9). The first of these responses summarize Jesus' posture toward the OT as God's Word: "But he answered, 'It is written, "Man shall not live by bread alone, but by every word that comes from the mouth of God"'" (Matthew 4:4; cf. Deuteronomy 8:3). God's Word is the source and sustenance of life (see Psalm 1:1–3; 119:25).

Fourth, Jesus sets up the expectation that His apostles would, by the aid of the Holy Spirit, authoritatively bear witness about who Jesus was and what He had done. Jesus prophesied of this before His crucifixion (John 15:26–27) and after (Acts 1:8). Additionally, in Luke 10:16 Jesus tells his disciples that "the one who hears you, hears me." In John 14:26 Jesus tells his followers, "the Holy Spirit, whom the Father will send in my name, he will teach you all things and bring to your remembrance all that I have said to you." Jesus' words in these passages are rightly applied to the disciples' later writings. He suggests that their writings will express His teaching, which indirectly implies that their works are inspired. Earlier we cited Luke 24:44–49. In these verses Jesus not only points to the inspiration of the OT in all its parts (Law, Prophets, and "Psalms"[12]), but He also declares that His apostles are witnesses to the fulfillment of the OT prophesies about Jesus (Luke 24:48) and that they will be empowered by the Holy Spirit ("the promise of my Father") to proclaim the good news of repentance and forgiveness of sins "to

---

[11] Luke 24:44 reads, "Then he said to them, 'These are my words that I spoke to you while I was still with you, that everything written about me in the Law of Moses and the Prophets and the Psalms must be fulfilled.'" The phrase "Law of Moses and the Prophets and the Psalms" is a way of referencing the Hebrew Bible (i.e., the Old Testament) in its entirety, since the Hebrew Scriptures were divided into three parts: Law, Prophets, and Writings (Psalms was the first book of the Writings).

[12] Law, Prophets, and Psalms (also called Writings) are the three divisions of the Hebrew Bible.

all nations" (cf. Luke 24:46). This is exactly what we find them doing in the book of Acts and across the remainder of the NT.

The View of the Apostles

What did the apostles teach about the Old and New Testament? Regarding the OT, the apostles' understanding of the OT aligned with Jesus'. Peter provides a foundational principle regarding the Scriptures that "no prophecy of Scripture (*graphē*) comes from someone's own interpretation. For no prophecy was ever produced by the will of man, but men spoke from God as they were carried along by the Holy Spirit" (2 Peter 1:20b–21 ESV). The term used for *Scripture* (*graphē*) is used here and regularly throughout the NT as a shorthand reference to the OT. This is the term used in 2 Timothy 3:16 when Paul declares, "All *Scripture* is breathed out by God" The apostles regularly cite and quote the OT Scriptures as fully inspired by God's Holy Spirit. But what did they think about their own writing?

Having been taught, commissioned, and empowered by the risen Christ to bear witness to His resurrection, the apostles understood themselves to be divinely commissioned and authoritative witnesses to Christ and His resurrection (Acts 1:22; 2:32; 3:15; 5:32; 10:39, 41; 13:31; 1 Peter 5:1; 1 Corinthians 15:15). We see this attitude reflected in how they refer to their apostolic writings as well.

To the Thessalonians, Paul writes, "And we also thank God constantly for this, that when you received the word of God, which you heard from us, you accepted it not as the word of men but as what it really is, the word of God, which is at work in you believers" (1 Thessalonians 2:13, ESV). To the Corinthians, Paul says that he, "in the sight of God," is "speaking in Christ" (2 Corinthians 12:19; 2:17) and that "Christ is speaking in me" (2 Corinthians 13:3). He reminds the Ephesians that the church is "built on the foundation of the apostles and prophets, Christ Jesus himself being the cornerstone" (Ephesians 2:20, ESV).

In the Gospel of John, the author (likely John the Apostle), declares his purpose in writing, "Now Jesus did many other signs in the presence of the disciples, which are not written in this book; but these are written so that you may believe that Jesus is the Christ, the Son of God, and that by believing you may have life in his name" (John 20:30–31, ESV). Commenting on the phrase "these are written" Ched Spellman notes, "In a book so careful about reserving the phrase, 'it is written' for quotations of authoritative writings (John 2:17; 6:31; 10:34; 15:25, etc.), this particular phrasing is brimming with theological import. The author locates this Gospel narrative as one of the sacred writings that enable and sustain life with God. From the author's perspective, then, this Gospel bears the full authority of the one who commissioned it, the risen Lord himself."[13]

But are the writings of the apostles rightly considered *Scripture* (*graphē*)? The apostle Peter references the letters of Paul and places them on the same level as the OT: "our beloved brother Paul also wrote to you according to the wisdom given him, as he does in all his letters when he speaks in them of these matters. There are some things in them that are hard to understand, which the ignorant and unstable twist to their own destruction, as they do the other Scriptures" (2 Peter 3:15b–16, ESV). Similarly, Paul places a quotation of Jesus found in the Gospels of Matthew and Luke on the same plane as teaching from the Book of Deuteronomy (see 1 Timothy 5:18; Matthew 10:10; Luke 10:7; Deuteronomy 24:15). So, we have at least two direct instances in which NT books were referred to as "Scripture."

We may be confronted by an objection. At the time when Paul was writing his letter to Timothy (A.D. mid-60s) the NT canon was not complete. For example, John's writings (i.e., the Gospel of John, 1–3 John, and Revelation) are all believed to have been written after Paul's death. Do these considerations mean that we

---

[13] Ched Spellman, "Bear with this Anonymous Exhortation: The Hermeneutical Effect of Anonymous Authorship for Readers of the New Testament," paper presented at the Ellis Foundation for Biblical Scholarship Conference at Lanier Theological Library, Houston, TX, May 19–21, 2022. Used with permission.

should have doubts about including John's writings in the category of Scripture? There is much to say on this topic (far more than we can tackle here). However, my response to this question is that we should have no trouble including John's writing or any other writings of the NT into the category of Scripture for all the reasons we listed earlier about the expectations that Jesus set up regarding the role of the apostles in providing witness to His resurrection. The same Spirit of God, the Spirit of Truth (John 15:26), who inspired the OT Scriptures (2 Peter 1:21) was breathed out upon Christ's disciples (John 20:22; Acts 2), filling and empowering them to remember all that Jesus had taught them (John 14:26) and proclaim with boldness (John 15:26–27; Acts 1:8) the good news of Christ and His resurrection. The apostles were commissioned eyewitnesses to the resurrection and therefore their writings are rightly considered part of the authoritative and trustworthy category of Christian Scripture.[14]

Conclusion

This chapter has sought to provide a foundation for thinking about the trustworthiness of God's Word (our Ancient Text). The goal was to outline the basic categories for explaining the trustworthiness of the biblical text. Central to our approach is locating the doctrine of Scripture within the doctrine of God. The oft-repeated phrase of the prophets "Thus says the LORD" is an appropriate description of what the Bible is as a whole: God's Word. As an instance of divine speaking, the Scriptures rise or fall based on the identity and character of this God. Further, as Christians, the doctrine of Scripture is grounded upon the definitive and final revelation of God in the person and work of Jesus Christ. In His preaching and teaching, Jesus consistently leaned upon the OT Scriptures to

---

[14] The topic of the Christian canon (i.e., authoritative collection of writings) is incredibly important and worthy of close attention. For a helpful introduction and overview of the relevant issues as well as a list of further resources to pursue on this topic see Ched Spellman, *One Holy Book: A Primer on How the Bible Came to Be & Why It Matters (Primers in Biblical and Theological Studies)* (Cedarville, OH: Codex Books, 2021).

validate the claims of both who He was and what He had come to do. Thus, to consider the trustworthiness of the Scripture is to at once consider the trustworthiness of Jesus and His teaching. The two questions cannot be untangled. Furthermore, we have sought to show that Jesus set up the expectation that His apostles would be the authoritative witnesses to His person and work (Luke 24:48) empowered by His Spirit for the evangelization of the world (Acts 1:8). Knowing that this ancient text of the Bible is sourced in the triune God declared within its pages, leads us to the conclusion that it is a text to be trusted. God's words are authoritative, effective, true, eternal, and good. As such, we find life when we delight ourselves in this book, and we cut ourselves off from life when we despise and neglect its truth.

This chapter has not dealt with other important questions related to the trustworthiness of Scripture. For example, we have not dealt with how the biblical writings were transmitted, how to think about the variations that appear in the manuscript traditions, the formation of the Christian canon of Scripture, or how to address specific, difficult passages in Scripture (e.g., that day when the sun reportedly stopped in the sky [Joshua 10:13]).[15] These issues are all related to defending the trustworthiness of Scripture, and there is much that can and must be said on these issues. That said, student ministers and students are best served by first appreciating the nature of the Bible in relation to the God to whom it attests. If it is in fact a self-revelation of this God (a God who is all-powerful, all-wise, trustworthy, etc.), then we have good reason to trust what it says. This foundational conviction will help sustain our trust in the text even as we engage some of the other important but more specific objections that the modern world may raise.

To round out our discussion, I'd like to offer several practical suggestions for fostering greater trust in the ancient text of the Bible:

---

[15] See the chapter footnotes for helpful resources for exploring these matters.

1. Teach the Scriptures. The degree to which you center your teaching ministry on the biblical text will communicate the level to which you trust the biblical text. Let the Scriptures be the foundation for the spiritual training you provide in your ministry. Your talks should be focused on expositing (i.e., exposing the meaning of) the biblical text. These are God's self-revealed and self-revealing words. These words are true and life-giving. What else do you have to offer students that the world doesn't already offer? Don't settle for something lesser.

2. Frame readings of the Scriptures with a reminder that these are the words of the Lord. I've heard pastors add a brief phrase such as "Hear the word of the Lord" or "This is the word of the Lord" before or after longer, public readings of Scripture. This is a minor move, but it has potentially strong, long-term effects on the hearers. It effectively does what we've labored to do in this chapter, it reminds people to listen to and think of the words of the Bible as God's words. You may have a different phrase you choose to use, but this subtle move will continually cement the foundation we've identified in this chapter.

3. Don't isolate the gospel from the larger canon of Scripture. Help your students see that the story of Jesus in the Gospels connects to all of the Bible on either side of the Gospels. As we have discussed in this chapter, this means that to accept Jesus as the Christ is to accept what Jesus said about the OT (it all bears truthful witness to him) and the NT (that the Holy Spirit would empower the apostles to bear truthful witness to him). This will help protect them from the idea that it is possible to accept Jesus and deny the trustworthiness of Scripture. Jesus tethered His defense of His identity as the Messiah to the trustworthiness of the OT and subsequently prophesied that his apostles would provide authoritative witness to Him. This approach will foster greater trust in the Bible.

4. Read the Scriptures publicly in times of worship, letting them prompt and shape services. Trust in the biblical canon is also reflected in our approach to worship. Joe Crider exhorts, "[S]elf-actuated worship is no more possible than self-actuated salvation. Worship leaders and worshipers may need to be reminded that we bring nothing to worship except a realization that by grace, through the power of the Holy Spirit, Jesus Christ is the only one who makes worship possible, and *our worship is a response to Him and His Word.*"[16] I love how Crider frames worship as a response to God's self-revelation in Scripture. If the Bible is God's self-revealed, inspired, infallible, inerrant/trustworthy, all-sufficient word to us, then our worship should be a response to it. These words and promises are true and sure, and these words should prompt and guide our worship.

---

[16] Joseph R. Crider, *Scripture-Guided Worship: A Call to Pastors & Worship Leaders* (Fort Worth: Seminary Hill Press, 2021), 15; emphasis added. Crider's book offers a stinging critique of a tendency in modern worship to neglect the public reading of God's Word as well as a failure to let our worship be a *response* to God's inerrant, all-sufficient word. I highly commend this practical and insightful book.

SECTION II

MODERN STUDENTS AND THEIR WORLD

The first year that I began growing crops in my backyard in Charleston, I had hardly any produce. Right down the road from us is a working farm and I could see their produce every time I drove by. Their produce was big, bright, and plentiful. I know I am not supposed to covet what my neighbor has, but I was coveting! I could not figure out why they had so much, and I had so little.

The next February, I drove by their farm and realized the farmers were working in the winter. They were working on the soil while I was just sitting in my house waiting for it to get warm enough to plant again. I realized the difference was their soil had been prepared for planting. I remembered when I was a teenager I would help my Grandad with his garden. Before we would plant, we would spend a week tilling the ground and getting it ready for planting. So, that spring before I planted, I bought new soil, rich with fertilizers, and worked the ground preparing it for planting. By summer, I had so much produce I had to give it away to my neighbors!

The soil our students live in has drastically changed. This section will examine modern students and their world. A major part of ministry to students is learning about the soil they live in so we can prepare them properly to receive the Word, our Ancient Text. If we only focus on the Ancient Text, we may be throwing seed out but it never takes root. This section will examine the modern world of a student. We will study the soil that our students live in, specifically in science, education, and culture. Once we understand the soil we are starting with, we can then begin preparing our students to hear the Ancient Text. In each of the topics of this section, we will also see how an Ancient Text still speaks into a modern world.

CHAPTER 6

THE WORLD OF A MODERN STUDENT

R. Allen Jackson, Ph.D.

Introduction

I was trolling one of my youth culture websites and came across this article:

> "No Emoji is Safe"
>
> What it is: Digital natives tend to use emoji less sincerely than their older counterparts, which makes for some confusion when it comes to the family group text.
>
> Why it's best to stick with words: As we've written about before, the "cry-laughing face" emoji has long been banned from the Gen Z-approved emoji lexicon. Now, as the Wall Street Journal reports, your emoji keyboard is practically a buffet of faux pas potential. That pained-looking frowny-face guy? He's what Gen Z uses to express desire, not frustration. And that smiley face emoji, once the most straightforward of fellows, is mostly interpreted by Gen Z as a passive-aggressive dig. (After all, nobody

looks that happy in real life.) You might want to ask your teen if your emoji-vocabulary needs some brushing up.[1]

Then I clicked over to Walt Mueller's website to inventory the most-surfed topics for parents, researchers, and even some students. In alphabetical order (and not the whole list), Abortion, Academic Pressure, Acceptance, Adoption, Age Aspiration, Anxiety, Body Image Pressure, Body Modification, Bullying, Cancel Culture, College, Contraception, Coronavirus, Cosmetic Surgery, Cutting, Cyberbullying Dating, Dating Violence, Electronic Addiction, Energy Drinks, Fake News, Families, Friends, Gambling, Gap Year, Hacking, Hazing, Hookup Culture, Human Trafficking, Identity, Influencers, Instagram, LGBTQ, Loneliness, Mental Health, Narcissism, Obesity, Online Gambling, Online Learning, Parenting, Pornography, Racism, Selfies, Sexting, Sexual Abuse, Social Media, Social Justice, TikTok, Tinder, Tumblr, Twitch, Twitter (the T's were fun), Unplug, Video Games, Vine, Virtual Reality, Wearables, Web Filters, YouTube and Zoom.[2]

I am overwhelmed—and I have taught youth culture for almost three decades. It changes so quickly. Dr. Mueller observed that youth culture books are obsolete by the time they are printed. When I taught youth culture, I looked at blogs, articles, websites, trend watch sources, and parent resources almost every day. As I look at many of those same resources today, I realize some things change and some things stay the same.

A Little Bit of History

Let's start with a short history of youth culture in the United States. Unlike animals, whose lifespan is mostly determined by biological makeup and instinctive processes, humans have the capacity to shape their social life in any manner they choose. We are created

---

[1] The Culture Translator, Vol. 7, Issue 34, August 20, 2021, Retrieved from https://axis.org/culture-translators/.

[2] Copied list from the resource page of CPYU, https://cpyu.org/resource_category/articles/.

in the image of a creative God. *Culture* refers to the world that humans build for themselves within a period in history and within a geographic location. Culture is the complex whole which includes knowledge, belief, art, morals, law, custom, and any other capabilities acquired by human beings as members of society."[3]

From a sociological point of view, there are elements and systems that make up a culture. Some are *material* (referring to the things we have) and some are *nonmaterial* (referring to the things we think or do). When politicians pass infrastructure bills, they are allegedly referring to highways, buildings, automobiles, internet grids, housing, and mass transit. Other systems include language (verbal, written, and symbols), and behavioral codes that range in enforcement from politeness to law to taboo.

Culture also includes government (authority, rulemaking, formal avenues to solve conflict); economy (trading goods and services), family structures, traditions, heroes, roles of individuals within the society, religion, and values. You can see why it took me a whole semester to teach a course on culture!

In the early 20th century, youth culture was born. I usually begin my adolescent development class with the question, "was adolescence discovered or invented?" My belief leans toward the *created* side, with a few factors specifically in mind. I acknowledge a bit of generalization, but prior to the 20th century and the Industrial Revolution, a typical family was more or less self-contained on a farm or in a city. Many children worked in the family business. For most of human history, a child became an adult. There was no in between phase of adolescence.

With the increasing migration from farm to city in the twentieth century and with technology reducing the need for raw numbers of workers, a few factors came together to create what we call adolescence. Jobs in factories needed to go to adults and around 1900, child labor laws were enacted. Shortly after, mandatory schooling

---

[3] Adapted from "What is Culture" in *The Promise of Sociology* by Ronald Fernandez (New York: Praeger Publishers, 1975) 33–34.

for children was legislated in several states, followed by the introduction of the juvenile justice system. The three had a cumulative effect of creating a time of moratorium between childhood and adulthood.

Couples were marrying later in life, rather than at sixteen or seventeen as was common in the previous century. "In short, it soon became apparent that a new stage of life—the TEENAGE phase—was becoming a reality in America. American adolescents were displaying traits unknown among children and adults. Although the word teenager did not come into use until decades later, the teenage mindset dawned in the 1920s."[4]

Perhaps the greatest contributor to the invention of adolescence and the subculture called teenagers was the automobile. Autonomy birthed freedom from parental oversight. The car was a *game-changer*. In a few paragraphs, I will talk about other game-changers in the youth culture.

The Christian Starting Line

Forbes Online contained a 2012 article by contributor Bill Flax that I found when I searched for "When America was Christian." Below you will find three paragraphs from the article with my commentary following each.[5]

> Few matters ignite more controversy than America's Christian roots. The issue reverberates anew this electoral season where the faiths of both major candidates have been questioned. Religion imbues politics. The battle over America's beginnings muddles wishful hero worship with efforts to commandeer America's past so to steer her future. The most vocal propo-

---

[4] U.S. History, *The Invention of the Teenager* Retrieved from https://www.ushistory.org/Us/46c.asp.

[5] Flax, B. (2012, September 25). *Was America Founded As A Christian Nation?* Retrieved from https://www.forbes.com/sites/billflax/2012/09/25/was-america-founded-as-a-christian-nation/.

nents of Christian America and their counterparts advocating a completely secular state necessarily cherry-pick data to prove exaggerations while discarding inconvenient details.

So the people, most of whom call themselves Christians, focus on the narrative that says that faith in Christ motivated the founding fathers to create a nation that would honor God, point to Jesus, and should be governed exclusively by biblical principles. While I don't think that is a bad idea (the last part about biblical principles), it is not historically accurate. The liberal voices likewise play fast and loose with the facts.

Meanwhile, those most ardently challenging America's Christian origins wrongly portray the Founders as rank secularists. They would seemingly reduce religious liberty to mere freedom of worship letting Believers pray in their hovels, but in public: Be seen and not heard. Some liberals seem inclined on expunging Christianity. Democrats nearly revolted over a fleeting reference to "God-given potential" at their convention.

What was accurate is that the founding fathers agreed with the last line as well. Biblical principles are character-shaping and character is what provides the nation with citizens who are able to look out for the greater good over that which exclusively benefits them.

The Founders disagreed on much, but were nearly unanimous concerning biblical morality. They understood the relationship between state and society differently than progressive thinkers today: government cannot mold man. Righteous men must mold government which requires the inculcation of virtue through vibrant churches and the transmittal of values generationally via a social structure based on families.

Lest you think I am off topic, remember that I am describing the world inhabited by students (and the rest of us as well). The narratives and counter-narratives in culture compete with biblical principles which coalesce into a biblical worldview. The prevailing worldview has resulted from the advance of secularism. The takeaway from that interaction is that while Christianity was assumed as foundational to the fabric of culture from the arrival of the Pilgrims until the midpoint of the twentieth century, that assumption is no longer valid. The Bible is not considered authoritative.

Trend Watching—Back to the Present

The adolescent experience was invented by culture. The industrial revolution with child labor laws and mandatory public schools provided extra leisure time or a *moratorium*. Youth culture further evolved with music, art, language, recreation that was esoteric to them—not necessarily shared with adults. Dating replaced courtship and eventually, sexuality replaced dating (the sexual revolution of the 1960s to the hookup culture of the 2000s).

The list of "what's hot and what's not" is constantly changing, and the world of students today is increasingly digital. A list of current trends would include TikTok, various platforms of social media that allow for self-expression, and technology. In addition to self-expression and communicating with friends, they have adapted to online shopping, entertainment, studying, peer interaction, and more. Youth pastors who used to say, "open your Bibles" now say, "swipe to John chapter three."

Online gaming dominates the attention span of many teenagers. Fortnite remains one of the leading multiplayer games and phone-based games are popular as well. YouTube and Netflix occupy hours upon hours of adolescent leisure time. Television shows are almost exclusively time-shifted. Trend watching topics could include food—increasingly organic and delivered through online apps; fashion—which changes rapidly and varies regionally, music, sports, hobbies; and even education. Virtual learning may be a game-changer, brought on by the COVID-19 pandemic.

Game-Changers

I define a game-changer as an invention, societal shift, or cultural event that completely change the way we live our lives. As opposed to fads (see above) that might fall into categories, but change rapidly, a game-changer means that we reset *normal* in a new place. The cell phone was a game-changer. We will never return to a world of landlines. The smart phone was even more of a game-changer. We are completely dependent on a personal computer for navigation, shopping, surfing, and communication through email, texting, and various apps. The bombing of the towers on September 11, 2001, was a game-changer. As a nation and as individuals, we will not return to a stress-free security experience at an airport or even a ball game. Online shopping was a game-changer as was virtual learning, social networking, food delivery apps, and even dating sites. Social networking changed the way we compare ourselves with others, Amazon changed the way we shop, texting changed the way we communicate, Siri changed the way we retain information (why remember it if I can just ask Siri?).

But even game-changers seem to operate within a sphere of principles that guide youth culture. Walt Mueller identified them as early as 1994:[6]

- The Cry of the Changing Family – changing definitions of family, divorce, mobile society, intact, blended, extended, single parent. Two working parents means that both male and female role models spend a majority of time away from the kids.

- The Cry of Moral Relativism – 68% of young people in this world believe that anything is true all of the time, majority of students do not assume biblical authority. I will speak more about cultural relativism below.

---

[6] Walt Mueller, *Understanding Today's Youth Culture* (Carol Stream, Il.: Tyndale Publishers, 1994). This was the first of several iterations of the book and the principles are summarized throughout. The commentary following the principle is my own. See also www.cypu.org.

- The Cry of Hopelessness – with social media, we have endless ways to compare ourselves to others. Many things have left students feeling so overwhelmed that hope is sometimes in short supply.

- The Cry of Media Influence – an undeniable and immeasurable aspect of the world of the modern teenager. See the game-changer discussion above.

From Cultural Relativism to a Post-Truth Culture

Moral relativism (postmodernity) and cultural relativism (we judge other cultures on the basis of our own) has taken an interesting turn. Students have been immersed in the notion that truth is a subjective construct, answering more to our own interpretation than objective reality. With regard to abortion, your body is yours to do with as you wish, or so we're told. You don't have to remain the gender of your birth. The same moral relativism is applied to sexual orientation and gender identity, euthanasia, and a host of other ethical issues.

Such relativism is infecting the church as well. Some studies have estimated that a majority of Christians under the age of 40 say Jesus is not the only way to salvation, claiming that Buddha and Muhammad are also valid paths to salvation.[7] I used to joke about postmodernism and its claims that no truth was absolute.

Would you want a postmodern banker?

Q: How much money do I have?

A: Enough.

Would you want a postmodern doctor?

Q: How bad is it, Doc?

A: Um, better than some, worse than others.

---

[7] Denison, J. 2021, August 25. "Will Your Taxes Soon Fund Abortions?" Retrieved from: https://www.denisonforum.org/daily-article/will-your-taxes-soon-fund-abortions/.

Silly, I know, but to deny that some things are simply objective is naive at best. To deny the evidence of God at work in creation, in redemption, in humanity is likewise short-sighted.

I now believe that postmodernity was a step toward what we are seeing today which is even more alarming. Welcome to a post-truth culture! We now live in a world where information flows instantly. Hardly any action or reaction escapes being filmed on someone's phone. The game-changers I talked about earlier have definitely reset the paradigm of culture around the world. Along with communication, a non-professional can alter images with digital tools, create from physical objects with 3-D printers, and manipulate data so that we look better than we might in real life.

What exactly is meant by the term *post-truth*? It has become a major buzz as postmodernity has evolved. As the 2016 Oxford English Dictionary's *Word of the Year* it is defined as the public burial of "objective facts" by an avalanche of media "appeals to emotion and personal belief."[8] In simpler terms, post-truth is embracing an idea or point of view on the basis of emotion rather than on the basis of objective facts. It shows up in political discourses, social discussions, and even around the family Thanksgiving table. It is exacerbated by social media and online blogs as well as biased *news* networks. It would be tempting to place the origin of the term to the contentious 2016 presidential election and subsequent term of President Trump, but that would ignore other highly charged incidents in which people on all sides of the issue reacted with angry and hateful partisan emotion, often ignoring facts in that did not support their position.

We have heard terms like *alternative facts*, *fake news*, and *felt truth*, all the while observing that more and more people are ready to ignore facts, eschew evidence, and willingly accept obvious lies. It would include *spin* or *selective memory* such as the omission of parts of a story that do not endorse a narrative we wish to embrace. In

---

[8] Oxford English Dictionary, 2nd ed. (Oxford: Oxford University Press, 2016), s.v. "post-truth."

very simple terms, "the facts don't really matter, only my feelings do."

In many ways, it is a natural outgrowth of relativism. Instead of absolute truth, there are only *personal truths*—subjective desires that shift with time, circumstance, or point of view. A claim that truth is universal, objective, or exclusive (especially in the case of Christianity) is increasingly met with scorn in the public arena or labeled as oppressive.

In this parallel universe, the feelings or preferences of an individual have been elevated to the place of highest authority. Don't like your birth gender? Claim another. Don't like someone's faith? Declare it as hate speech. Don't like the way an election turned out? Claim it was stolen. Don't want to get vaccinated? Go to YouTube to find an expert who supports your point of view. I could go on, and I intentionally cited a couple of examples that you as the reader might find offensive. That's the point. Emotion-based truth ends up being woven into the fabric of our identity. Perhaps saddest of all is that to merely disagree with another's *personal truth* is considered to be an act of hatred. If you don't agree with me, I cannot *agree to disagree*. Instead, I must label you an enemy. The church is not immune. We have disagreed over many issues and in our world today, the result is often speech or behavior that is anything but Christ-honoring.

Jesus did not place feelings ahead of truth. In His famous conversation with Pilate in John 18:38, He confronted the world's definition of truth. He told the disciples that they could and would know the truth, and that the truth would set them free (John 8:32). He claimed to be the way, the truth, and the life (John 14:6). Truth was a person, a person who lived, breathed, taught, was crucified, and buried—and rose from the dead. He—Truth—is knowable, objective, and absolute. God is who He is, not who we might imagine or want Him to be.

A Personal Word to Close

On August 29, 2005, my world changed. Hurricane Katrina blew through New Orleans and left between three and five feet of water in my house, rendering it uninhabitable. I have observed first-hand how teenagers—including my own—have been shaped by some of the worldview influences described in this paper. Each day has been a challenge—new schools, new home, new friends, new food chain, etc. I am surprised to see so many youth deal with the aftermath of such a radical invasion on their lives with secular rather than spiritual outlook. While many volunteer to help others, many others have demonstrated that spiritual solutions are for spiritual problems (my friend needs to be saved or my grandfather is sick) but secular problems have secular solutions (I got in a fight at school because the kids in Baton Rouge said something bad about New Orleans).

With my own teenagers, teaching critical thinking skills has been an uphill climb. The immediacy of alleviating pain often overshadows ongoing consequences. At times, it seems as if the need for survival pushes the thought of worldview development into the background. Upon further contemplation, I realized that the whole point of worldview formation is that it becomes part of the tapestry of unconscious thought. If a Christian worldview is cultivated when the storms are not blowing, then it provides a framework for survival after the storm. We need to pray for our kids that as we "train them up in the way they should go" they can see the connection between the theoretical and the pragmatic—the thought life of redemption and the "as you go" of the Great Commission.

Of course, the ultimate expression of God's truth is found in the gospel—not a feeling or a subjective belief, but an unchangeable historical event through which God reconciled the world to Himself. No one can deny that feelings are part of the way God made us, but they are designed to respond to the truth and be shaped by it, not the other way around.

CHAPTER 7

ANCIENT TEXT, MODERN SCIENCE

Ross Parker, Ph.D.

Introduction

Contemporary students have grown up in a post-truth and post-Christian context. This context comes through specifically in how contemporary culture thinks about the relationship between science and Christian Scripture. Students today are bombarded with statements about this relationship (or the supposed lack of relationship). Here are three slogans that are common in our culture—I'm confident that most students have heard some version of all three of these claims:

1) "Christianity is committed to believing without evidence, but science gives us knowledge based on evidence."

2) "Christianity is anti-science."

3) "Modern science has shown that Christian Scripture is false."

These views, and others like them, have become a part of the un-questioned assumptions in many contexts of our daily lives. And these assumptions impact students in our churches.[1]

As Christians, we are called to engage in spiritual warfare. In this spiritual warfare, the Apostle Paul calls us to engage with ideas that stand opposed to God's truth. Second Corinthians 10:3–5 says, "For though we walk in the flesh, we are not waging war according to the flesh. For the weapons of our warfare are not of the flesh but have divine power to destroy strongholds. *We destroy arguments and every lofty opinion raised against the knowledge of God, and take every thought captive to obey Christ*" (ESV, emphasis added).

We need to help students see that each of these claims doesn't hold up to rational scrutiny. In the rest of this chapter, I want to provide an analysis of each of these slogans to equip you to help students combat these errors. Students need to see that the truth we discover through science and the truth that we discover through Scripture are in concord, not in conflict.

Slogan #1

Consider the first slogan: *Christianity is committed to believing without evidence, but science gives us knowledge based on evidence.*

This slogan makes a claim about Christianity, and it makes a claim about science. Let's start with the first part of the claim—*Christianity is committed to believing without evidence.* This claim is rooted in a common view about the nature of faith known as *fideism*. Fideism is the view that faith is believing something without evidence. Christians obviously think that we should have faith, so if you think that faith is believing something without evidence, then the first part of this claim would be true.

---

[1] To give just one example, in the Faith That Lasts Project, a survey of young adults who regu-larly attended church in their teen years found that 25% accept the statement "Christianity is anti-science." See "Six Reasons Young Christians Leave Church," September 27, 2011, re-trieved from https://www.barna.com/research/six-reasons-young-christians-leave-church/.

I don't think fideism adequately describes biblical faith. For support of this claim, consider Jesus' response when John the Baptist sent two of his disciples to ask Jesus the question "Are you the one who is to come, or shall we look for another?" (Matthew 11:3, ESV). If biblical faith is believing without evidence, then wouldn't Jesus say something like "just believe that I'm the Messiah"? But that is not Jesus' response. Jesus responds in this way: "Go and tell John what you hear and see: the blind receive their sight and the lame walk, lepers are cleansed and the deaf hear, and the dead are raised up, and the poor have good news preached to them" (Matthew 11:4-5, ESV). Jesus points to the evidence of what He is doing in His ministry and how His actions fulfill the prophecies about the Messiah found in Isaiah (see Isaiah 26:19; 29:18-19; 35:5-6; 53:4).

There are many other biblical examples we could give showing that biblical faith is not believing without evidence. Consider Paul's proclamation of the gospel on his missionary journeys. Here's how Luke describes Paul's ministry when he came to Thessalonica:

> They came to Thessalonica, where there was a synagogue of the Jews. And Paul went in, as was his custom, and on three Sabbath days he reasoned with them from the Scriptures, explaining and proving that it was necessary for the Christ to suffer and to rise from the dead, and saying, "This Jesus, whom I proclaim to you, is the Christ" (Acts 17:1-3, ESV).

Rather than *belief without evidence*, we should understand biblical faith as *trusting in God*. More specifically, saving faith is trusting in Jesus and His salvific work on our behalf.[2] This trust in God and His salvific work can and should be based on good evidence. Consider everyday examples of the way we use the term *faith*. I have

---

[2] For helpful discussions of biblical faith, see the following: Thomas A. Howe and Richard G. Howe, "Knowing Christianity Is True: The Relationship Between Faith and Reason," in *To Everyone An Answer: A Case for the Christian Worldview*, ed. Francis J. Beckwith, William Lane Craig, and J. P. Moreland (Downers Grove, IL: IVP Academic, 2004), 23–36; J. P. Moreland and Klaus Issler, *In Search of a Confident Faith: Overcoming Barriers to Trusting in God* (Downers Grove, IL: IVP Books, 2008), Chapter 1 "What Faith Is… and What It Isn't."

faith in my wife because I trust my wife; I trust her because I have good reasons to believe that she is trustworthy. Theologian Wayne Grudem, in his discussion of the biblical account of faith, goes so far as to make the following claim: "Because saving faith in Scripture involves ... personal trust, the word 'trust' is a better word to use in contemporary culture than the word 'faith' or 'belief.'"[3] If *trusting in God* is the right account of biblical faith, then Christians are not committed to believing things without evidence.

Now consider the second part of this slogan: *science gives us knowledge based on evidence.* A Christian should not have a problem with this statement taken at face value. The physical sciences can give us knowledge about our world based on evidence. But when this statement is presented as a part of this slogan, there are often serious errors behind it.

Potential Error #1: The sentiment that science gives us knowledge because it is based on evidence, whereas this is not the case for Christianity, is often rooted in a view that the *only* way we can know something is by *empirical* evidence. This is a view about how we know called *scientism.* The proponent of scientism thinks that what we can know is limited to what can be empirically verified. Since you can't empirically verify that God exists, and you can't empirically verify that the Bible is God's Word, then you can't know these things.

But scientism is clearly a bad approach to knowledge. First, scientism is self-defeating. A statement is self-defeating if the statement proves itself false. For example, if I say, "I don't exist," my statement is self-defeating (since I must exist to make the statement). So how is scientism self-defeating? We can state the position of scientism as: *The only statements you can know are those statements that can be empirically verified.* Then we apply this statement to itself. This statement doesn't seem like it could possibly be empirically verified. There's no sensory evidence for the principle *The only*

---

[3] Wayne Grudem, *Systematic Theology: An Introduction to Biblical Doctrine*, Second edition (Grand Rapids, MI: Zondervan, 2020), 862.

statements that you can know are statements that can be empirically verified. So that means that we can't know that scientism is true, which is a serious problem for scientism.[4]

Second, scientism is a much too narrow view of knowledge. To take an everyday example, I know that the statement: "I ate a peanut butter and jelly sandwich for lunch yesterday." is true. And while perhaps this statement could be supported based on empirical evidence (we could go through my trash can and find the leftover crust, etc.), my knowledge is not based on any empirical evidence— my memory of eating the sandwich yesterday is sufficient. Considering these two problems, if this slogan is motivated by scientism, then the slogan should be rejected along with this false approach to knowledge.

Potential Error #2: Another potential problem with this slogan is that it might be based on a view that claims science rests on a surer foundation than other knowledge claims because it sticks with what is directly verifiable with our senses. If this is what undergirds this slogan, we need to help students see that this is a naïve view of science. Scientific knowledge goes beyond what is directly empirically verifiable. To take a simple example, we can't directly empirically verify gravity—what we empirically verify is a phenomenon like apples falling from trees. From the phenomenon, we *infer* the law of gravity. Quarks are sub-atomic particles that are not empirically verifiable. Their existence is inferred from the phenomenon that scientists observe. We cannot directly empirically experience the cause of a crater because it's an event that happened in the past, but we can infer the cause scientifically. Many other examples could be given of things we take to be items of scientific knowledge that aren't directly empirically verifiable.

---

[4] There are many helpful discussions of the inadequacies of scientism. For a helpful place to start see Paul Copan, *How Do You Know You're Not Wrong?: Responding to Objections That Leave Christians Speechless* (Grand Rapids, MI: Baker Books, 2005), Chapter 4 "Unless You Can Scientifically Verify or Falsify Your Belief, It's Meaningless" and Chapter 5 "You Can't Prove That Scientifically." For an important book-length treatment, see J. P. Moreland, *Scientism and Secularism: Learning to Respond to a Dangerous Ideology* (Crossway, 2018).

Hopefully this brief discussion has shown the problems with the slogan "Christianity is committed to believing without evidence, but science gives us knowledge based on evidence." Christianity is not based on belief without evidence. We are called to trust God, and that trust should be rooted in evidence-based Christian world-view beliefs. Also, empirical evidence isn't the only way we can know things, and science itself extends beyond what is directly empirical.

Slogan #2

Let's now turn our attention to the second slogan: *"Christianity is anti-science."* I do not think I need to provide much evidence for this being a common sentiment that students today hear and encounter regularly. We need to help students see that this statement is simply not true.

My first point is simple, but it shows the inadequacy of this slogan. If Christianity is genuinely anti-science, then faithful Christians could not be successful scientists. But we can look at the history of science to see that many of the greatest scientists have been Christians—and they have seen their scientific work as supported by their Christian faith. Here are just a few examples. First Galileo Galilei (1564–1642) is a giant in the history of science; he made foundational contributions to the science of motion and astronomy. Galileo saw his scientific endeavors and his Christian faith as fitting together. According to Pearcey and Thaxton, "Galileo's behavior cannot be understood unless we accept his own claim that he was a believer and that he placed religion alongside science as a source of genuine information about the world."[5] Another example is Robert Boyle (1627–1691), who discovered the relationship between the pressure and volume of a gas that became known as "Boyle's Law." He is recognized as one of the innovators of the experimental method. Boyle was a committed Christian, and his faith

---

[5] Nancy R. Pearcey and Charles B. Thaxton, *The Soul of Science: Christian Faith and Natural Philosophy* (Wheaton, IL: Crossway Books, 1994), 40.

in Christ was central to his scientific endeavors.[6] We can add many other names to this list. For a recent example, Francis Collins has served as director of the National Human Genome Research Institute and has made important discoveries about disease genes. He recently finished his service as the director of the National Institutes of Health. Collins is also a committed Christian—see his book *The Language of God.*

But more fundamentally, the Christian worldview actually *supports* science; it provides the foundations for science in ways that no other worldview does. Science can only flourish in the context of certain pre-scientific commitments. In other words, there are certain presuppositions of science that must be assumed when we do science.[7] Empirical science developed as an independent discipline in Europe in the 16th and 17th centuries in what is referred to as "the Scientific Revolution."[8] Scholars have noted that 16th-century Europe was not the most advanced culture in terms of knowledge at this time (Muslim culture and the Chinese culture was more advanced in various areas).[9] Yet it was in Europe where science developed as a discipline, and many scholars have noted that it was the broadly Christian intellectual commitments that led to the development of science.[10] I want to highlight two of these pre-scientific commitments and point to their clear connection to a Christian worldview. I'll also briefly point out how these foundations don't fit well in a naturalistic worldview.

---

[6] See the discussion of Boyle's faith in Michael Hunter, "Robert Boyle," in *Oxford Dictionary of National Biography* (Oxford: Oxford University Press, 2004), 106.

[7] For a helpful discussions of this point, see the following: Steven B. Cowan and James S. Spiegel, *The Love of Wisdom: A Christian Introduction to Philosophy* (Nashville, TN: B&H Academic, 2009), 105–6; J. P. Moreland, *Christianity and the Nature of Science: A Philosophical Investigation* (Grand Rapids, MI: Baker, 1989), 108–33; Pearcey and Thaxton, *The Soul of Science*, 21–36.

[8] See the discussion in J. Brookes Spencer, Margaret J. Osler, and Stephen G. Brush, "Scientific Revolution," in *Encyclopedia Britannica*, accessed September 17, 2021, https://academic.eb.com/levels/collegiate/article/Scientific-Revolution/631832.

[9] See Pearcey and Thaxton, *The Soul of Science*, 21.

[10] For more on this, see Rodney Stark, *How the West Won: The Neglected Story of the Triumph of Modernity* (Wilmington, DE: ISI Books, 2014), Ch. 15 "Science Comes of Age."

First, science depends on the assumption that the universe is governed by natural laws. One of the things that science does is seek to find the laws that govern the workings of the physical world. But why think that all physical reality across all time and space will work according to general physical laws? This is something that is assumed rather than proved. This assumption fits naturally in a biblical worldview. Christianity affirms that the physical world was created by a rational God. If you think that God is rational, then it makes sense to think that His universe will be governed by regularities. But what if you think that there is no reasonable creator God? The implication would be that the universe is mindless and directionless. In that case, it *might* be true that the physical stuff of the universe behaves in the same way across time and space, but it seems like that might *not* be the case as well.

Second, science also depends on the assumption that humans can discover truths about nature. Why engage in studying the natural world unless we think that we will have success? We engage in science *assuming* that we will be able to learn more about the natural world. This assumption fits well with Christianity. According to Christianity, we are created in the image of God, and as such God created us as capable of learning about the world he created. So, seeking to learn more about the world fits with the Christian worldview. But atheism implies that ultimately, human cognitive faculties developed so that we could survive and pass on our genes. Many thinkers have pointed out that if this is so, we should not be confident that our cognitive systems get us at the truth.[11] Further, even if our cognitive systems are accurate in getting everyday truths (like "eating this apple will not poison me; it will nourish me"), why think that they would be reliable in figuring out the laws

---

[11] For more in-depth discussion of this point see the following discussions: C. S. Lewis, *Miracles: A Preliminary Study*, Revised Edition (1960; repr., New York: Simon & Schuster, 1996), Ch. 3 "The Cardinal Difficulty of Naturalism"; Alvin Plantinga, *Where the Conflict Really Lies: Science, Religion, and Naturalism* (Oxford: Oxford University Press, 2011), Ch. 10 "The Evolutionary Argument Against Naturalism."

that govern sub-atomic reality (to take one example) when that doesn't seem to help us survive and pass on genes?

Slogan #3

We can now consider the third slogan—*"Modern science has shown that the Bible is false."* I want to briefly make three points in response to this slogan.

First, when there's a claim that a finding of science conflicts with Scripture, we need to distinguish between 1) what the Bible *actually* says, and 2) our *interpretation* of what the Bible says. It may be that the scientific finding is only in conflict with our interpretation of the Bible. Let me give an example. In the past, many Christians claimed the Bible taught that the sun and planets revolved around the earth. For example, Martin Luther (1483–1546) critiqued the heliocentric model of Copernicus for being unbiblical. He thought the Bible clearly taught geocentrism—for example, Joshua told the Sun to stand still (see Joshua 12). But no Christians I know of are still trying to defend the view that the sun revolves around the earth. Christians have come to recognize that the Bible does not teach a geocentric view. Rather, it describes things as they appear. My point is that there may be places where the conflict between modern scientific findings and the Bible is actually a conflict with an *interpretation* of the Bible.

Second, I want to note that the findings of science don't have a great track record of holding over time. If we look at the history of science, there have been many theories and laws that were taken as the settled findings of science, but which turn out to be false. Consider Newton's law of gravitation, to take one example. This was accepted for a long time, but Einstein's general theory of relativity showed that Newton's law of gravitation isn't a universal law.[12] And even with Einstein's theory, scientists now think that his account of

---

[12] David Lyth, "How Einstein's general theory of relativity killed off common-sense physics," *The Conversation*, November 24, 2015. Retrieved from https://theconversation.com/how-einsteins-general-theory-of-relativity-killed-off-common-sense-physics-50042.

gravity doesn't hold in a black hole.[13] This data can ground a "pessimistic induction" (to use the terminology of the contemporary philosophical argument I'm referring to).

1) Many past scientific theories that were empirically supported and now recognized to be false.

So ...

2) Today's scientific theories will probably be recognized as false in the future.

I'm not claiming that this argument undermines all scientific claims. I think that we're making progress in understanding the world. But it seems that science's track record justifies a legitimate hesitancy in accepting scientific theories when they are relatively recent. So if a contemporary scientific theory seems to be in conflict with what the Bible teaches, it very well could be that the scientific theory will turn out to be superseded by a new theory in the future.

Third, there are several instances where modern science has given evidence *for* biblical truth. Here's the first example. The Bible affirms that God made all things out of nothing (*ex nihilo*). The implication of this doctrine is that the physical universe is not eternal—it came into existence at creation. Historically, naturalism (as well as many other non-Christian worldviews) asserts that the material world is eternal. But (to simplify matters) in the early part of the 20th-century scientific discoveries have pointed to the conclusion that the universe came into being at a finite point in the past.[14] This conclusion was resisted by some scientists because they recognized the creationist implications of this conclusion.

---

[13] From Jeremy Deaton "Einstein showed Newton was wrong about gravity. Now scientists are coming for Einstein." https://www.nbcnews.com/mach/science/einstein-showed-newton-was-wrong-about-gravity-now-scientists-are-ncna1038671.

[14] If you want to look at this scientific evidence, consult various defenses of the Kalam Cosmological Argument in the Christian Apologetics literature. See, for example, William Lane Craig, *On Guard: Defending Your Faith With Reason and Precision* (Colorado Springs, CO: David C. Cook, 2010), Ch. 4 "Why Did the Universe Begin?"; R. Douglas Geivett, "The Kalam Cosmological Argument," in *To Everyone An Answer: A Case for the Christian Worldview*, ed. Francis J. Beckwith, William Lane Craig, and J. P. Moreland (Downers Grove, IL: IVP Academic, 2004), 61–76.

Here's a second example. As scientists have come to understand what is required for there to be a universe where life is even *possible*, they have identified that a number of cosmological constants and quantities have to be in a very narrow range for a life-permitting universe. This is referred to as the phenomenon of *fine-tuning* for life.

Here are just two examples of fine-tuning. According to scientist Paul Davies, there is an "almost unbelievable delicacy in the balance between gravity and electromagnetism within a star. Calculations show that changes in the strength of either force by only one part in 10^{40} would spell catastrophe for stars like the sun."[15] William Lane Craig states that "the so-called *weak force*, one of the four fundamental forces of nature, which operates inside the nucleus of an atom, is so finely tuned that an alteration in its value by even one part out of 10^{100} would have prevented a life-permitting universe!"[16] There are many more we could list here. Each example gives a fundamental constant or quantity that is in a narrow life-permitting range. But when you look at them together, that they are all in the life-permitting range becomes *incredibly* unlikely. These constants and quantities seem like they could have been other than they are. That they are so well balanced to support life is incredibly surprising if naturalism is true. But these scientific findings support the biblical view that the universe was created by God to support the life that He created.[17]

---

[15] Paul Davies, *Superforce: The Search for a Grand Unified Theory of Nature* (New York: Simon & Schuster, 1985), 242.

[16] Craig, *On Guard: Defending Your Faith With Reason and Precision*, 109.

[17] The point of this paragraph can be developed into a more robust argument for God. For helpful discussions, see the following: Robin Collins, "A Scientific Argument for the Existence of God: The Fine-Tuning Argument," in *Reason for the Hope Within*, ed. Michael J. Murray (Grand Rapids, MI: Eerdmans, 1999), 47–75; Craig, *On Guard: Defending Your Faith With Reason and Precision*, Ch. 5, "Why Is the Universe Fine-Tuned for Life?"

Conclusion

Students today are bombarded with claims that aim to drive a wedge between biblical truth and science. But while these slogans have popular appeal, they simply don't get the relationship between biblical Christianity and science right. Let's help students have a more accurate view of this relationship, recognizing that, as the Belgic Confession says, "The universe is before our eyes like a beautiful book in which all creatures, great and small, are as letters to make us ponder the invisible things of God." Let's help today's students see that all truth comes from God, whether He reveals it in nature as a part of general revelation or in Scripture as a part of special revelation.

CHAPTER 8

ANCIENT TEXT AND GLOBALIZING CULTURES

Ryan Gimple, Ph.D.

Youth stand on the front edge of the wave of cultural change. When youth come of age, the new generation pushes their culture into its future. Youth are part of the cultural current, but they are on the leading edge of that current, with the wave of societal cultural pressures pushing them into their own new and changing cultural expression.

All across the globe, we have become increasingly aware of the magnificent cultural diversity of humanity. The massive amount of migration over the past century has brought most of us into contact with others of diverse languages and cultures. Transportation and technological changes have facilitated an awareness of other cultures, a mixing and sharing between cultures. Urbanization has also brought diverse peoples into a shared space. There has been a movement toward a shared global culture (globalization) as well as a pulling back from global culture into differentiated local cultures (glocalization). All cultures are in the midst of this push and pull, like the tides on an ocean.

Culture and language are interrelated. Culture and language can be differentiated but not separated—like the surface of the ocean from the currents flowing below. There are more than 7,000 languages spoken today in our world. Half of humanity speaks 23 of these languages, while approximately 3,000 of the languages in the world are endangered and have no more than a few thousand speakers.[1] Within the major language groups, there are yet a variety of cultural forms. Language is a primary element shaping a culture, but the diversity of our globe goes deeper than differences in language. How do the words of the ancient text of the Bible relate to the diverse cultures around the globe today? The Bible is a text from a different time and different culture. When Christians say that the words of the Bible are true, are we only trying to impose our culture on the culture of others in a form of cultural aggression? Don't the ancient words just hold us back from the progress and direction of our culture? How do the words of the Bible relate to the multitude of cultures around us?

Let's approach cultural diversity first by looking at what the Bible tells us about diversity. The Bible reveals to us that God is a God of diversity. In the first few words of the book of Genesis, God reveals that He values diversity in His creation. He does not create a homogenous world, but one in which there is a multitude of plants and animals differentiated according to their kinds. When I step outside my insulated home into nature and sit still while listening and looking, the diverse biological world God created reveals itself. God does not let diversity in nature perish due to human wickedness, but He saves the diversity of His creation through the flood in Genesis 6–9. God initiated human cultural diversity as He scattered the many differentiated nations and languages in Genesis 10–11. The cultural diversity we see in the world today is not something that is against God's plan and design, but the God of the Bible is the Creator and Lord and Savior of diversity. Culture results from cooperative human effort to fulfill the mandate of Genesis 1:26. If God

---

[1] "How Many Languages Are There in the World?" Ethnologue, Retrieved April 2, 2022, from https://www.ethnologue.com/guides/how-many-languages.

is the creator of diversity, then diversity is something we should value and protect in our cultural endeavors. We honor God through cultural diversity. Diversity divides only because of the warping of sin, not because of anything inherent in diversity. In God's being and His creational design, diversity and unity are equal partners. The doctrine of the Trinity helps us to see how diversity and unity cohere.

The term *culture* requires a definition. It is obvious we are not talking about yogurt or Petri dishes, and we are also not talking about culture in the sense of being well-educated. Christian missiologists and anthropologists have previously written much on culture and we can borrow from their conceptions. Charles Kraft explains, "The term 'culture' is the label anthropologists give to the structured customs and underlying worldview assumptions which govern people's lives."[2] Kraft differentiates between the surface-level culture of patterned behavior, material artifacts, and what we habitually do, think, and feel, from the deep-level culture which contains our worldview assumptions that govern the surface level culture. Kraft makes this division to show that cultural change agents should not attempt to change the surface level of culture without attending to the deep-culture structures. Lloyd E. Kwast in "Understanding Culture" describes culture as a series of layers.[3] The outer layer is the patterns of behavior. Below that layer are values of what is good or best. The next layer deeper is the layer of beliefs expressing what is true. The very center at the core of culture is worldview that encompasses the ultimate questions regarding reality. Both Kraft and Kwast present layered models of culture that view some aspects of culture as being visible on the surface, but the more important area of culture is under the surface. Paul Hiebert's definition of culture is one of the clearest definitions of culture from an evangelical

---

[2] Charles H. Kraft, "Culture, Worldview, and Contextualization," in *Perspectives on the World Christian Movement: A Reader*, 3rd ed. (Pasadena, CA: William Carey Library, 1999), 384–91.

[3] Lloyd E. Kwast, "Understanding Culture," in *Perspectives on the World Christian Movement: A Reader*, ed. Ralph D Winter and Steven C Hawthorne, 4th ed. (Pasadena, CA: William Carey Library, 2009), 397–99.

anthropologist. Hiebert defines culture as "the more or less integrated systems of ideas, feelings, and values and their associated patterns of behavior and products shared by a group of people who organize and regulate what they think feel, and do."[4] Culture has internal aspects (ideas, feelings, and values) as well as external aspects (patterns of behavior and products). Culture is not something that belongs to an individual, but it is shared between a group of people. Any given individual both is *shaped by* and *a shaper of* the surrounding culture. In our multi-cultural age, individuals are simultaneously shaping and being shaped by multiple overlapping cultural communities.

Cultures should not be thought of as static or rigidly bounded. Cultures are not isolated pools. Arjun Appadurai discusses culture as being made of "cultural flows." In "Disjuncture and Difference in the Global Cultural Economy" Appadurai describes cultural flows that cross five types of landscape: mediascape, financescape, ideoscape, ethnoscape, and technoscape.[5] Culture never stays in one place, but is always moving. Glaciers are always flowing and moving, albeit very slowly, so that it is difficult to perceive without measurement. Culture and language sometimes change slowly enough that we do not easily perceive the change.

The English language of our present year does not seem so different from a year or two ago, but there has been movement. The movement is easier to see when you look at the flow over a longer period of time. When reading Shakespeare the cultural-linguistic difference becomes more apparent. The language and ideas in Shakespeare continue to influence our language and culture today and we are part of the same langua-cultural stream, but we are far downstream. We are part of the same language and cultural flow,

---

4 Paul G. Hiebert, *Anthropological Insights for Missionaries* (Grand Rapids, MI: Baker Book House, 1985), 30.

5 Arjun Appadurai, *Modernity at Large: Cultural Dimensions of Globalization* (Minneapolis, MN: University of Minnesota Press, 1996), https://ebookcentral.proquest.com/lib/csuniv/reader.action?docID=310379&ppg=7; Arjun Appadurai, "Disjuncture and Difference in the Global Cultural Economy," Theory, Culture & Society 7, no. 2–3 (June 1990): 295–310, https://doi.org/10.1177/026327690007002017.

but the language and culture are in a different place now. Like glaciers, the world's cultures and languages have been slowly moving.

The global *technoscape* has been rapidly changing. Fifteenth-century maritime innovations made possible the discovery of new lands and the collisions of various cultures which otherwise would not have rubbed shoulders. As cultures collide, the interaction changes both, just as when two flowing currents meet. The invention of the printing press fueled cultural change and sped up the flow and exchange. The rate of cultural change spurred on by the age of exploration and the printing press has exponentially increased in the past century with the development of the airliner and the internet. Information, language, and culture can now be instantaneously transmitted worldwide. Global cultures today resemble whitewater rapids more so than glaciers. They are not just flowing, they are swirling and fomenting, and the youth are on the crest of the wave.

Cultural forms and messages move quickly across the globe. Consider the development of hip-hop. Hip-hop finds its origins in nightclubs in New York City in the early 1970s as DJs began improvising and rapping while changing records. Eventually it was the DJs rap that the crowd looked forward to. The first rap album, Rapper's Delight, was recorded and released by the Sugarhill Gang in 1979. Rap music spread primarily in America's urban centers, New York, Philadelphia, Detroit, and Los Angeles, and it was developed primarily by African-Americans. Hip-hop could not be confined to one city or culture, and it was adopted by other forms and other cultures.[6] MC Jin is a Chinese American rap artist who raps in English, Mandarin, and Cantonese, having performed regularly in Hong Kong, but also having toured Mainland China. Since his conversion to Jesus in 2013, MC Jin's recent rap is infused with his faith in Jesus. Jin's music is a case study that makes visible a rapidly moving and boundary breaking flow of culture, and also shows us that the good news of Jesus can also enter into diverse cultural forms, and forms

---

[6] H. Samy Alim, Awad Ibrahim, and Alastair Pennycook, eds., *Global Linguistic Flows: Hip Hop Cultures, Youth Identities, and the Politics of Language* (New York, NY: Routledge, 2009).

that are themselves on the move. If the Word of God can influence, be expressed by, and transform Chinese Hip-Hop, what cultural form can you throw at it that it cannot enter?

But how can an ancient text like the Bible stay afloat and compete with the changing forms and ideas as they quickly flow and foment across the rapidly changing global cultural scapes? Isn't the Bible just promoting one cultural form, an imperialistic pushing of an ancient culture, and one that has not to hope for survival in our present pluralistic cultural moment? Can the Bible be translated into the changing language-cultural forms of our day and still remain the Word of God?

The Bible is translatable in every single one of the rapidly flowing langua-cultures of our world. God's mission proceeds through His action of translating His Word. Andrew Walls describes the "The Translation Principle in Christian History" in *The Missionary Movement in Christian History: Studies in the Transmission of Faith*.[7] Walls notes that the first act of divine translation can be seen in the incarnation. "Incarnation is translation. When God in Christ became man, Divinity was translated into humanity, as though humanity were a receptor language.... He became a *person* in a particular locality and in a particular ethnic group, at a particular place and time"[8] When God became man, the Word entered into a particular culture, time, and language, becoming visible and palpable. The eternal Word could be heard, seen, and touched (1 John 1:1-5). Jesus is the central act of divine translation, but the translation principle is found first in the Old Testament.

The Bible crosses languages and cultures even within itself. God judged the Hebrew people in the Old Testament by scattering them in exile to Babylon. Daniel and Ezra wrote during the return from exile. Most of the Old Testament is written in Hebrew, but Ezra and Daniel each contain some passages written in Aramaic. Aramaic

---

[7] Andrew F. Walls, *The Missionary Movement in Christian History: Studies in the Transmission of Faith* (Maryknoll, New York: Orbis Books, 1996).

[8] Walls, 27; Frank O'Hara, "Incarnation as Translation," *New Blackfriars* 52, no. 616 (1971): 417–22.

was a common trade language that was used to communicate with people of other nations during the Babylonian exile. In Ezra and Daniel, God revealed that He is a God of all cultures and languages by using Aramaic language. God's Word was not ever meant to be confined to Hebrew. He reveals His word cross-linguistically and cross-culturally.

Further, God shows that His Word is translatable through another act before the time of Jesus. After Alexander the Great (356 BC–323 BC), Greek culture and language spread among many cultures, and the Hebrew Scriptures were translated into Greek. The Greek translation is affirmed as God's Word just as certainly as the Hebrew original. In Luke 4, Jesus reads from Isaiah in the synagogue, and He is reading from the Greek translation.[9] Jesus affirms the Greek translation. Scripture itself gives us evidence that God affirms the translation of His Word into other languages. God inspires the various authors of the New Testament to write in Greek. The God of the Bible is not confined to one culture or language but revealed Himself to us in three languages internal to Scripture itself. The Bible is inherently a cross-cultural book.

The book of Acts makes it clear that the Holy Spirit does not intend for His Word to remain in Hebrew, Aramaic, or Greek, but in Acts 2, He empowers the apostles to communicate the good news of Jesus in a plethora of languages, and in 1 Corinthians 12:10, speaking and interpreting languages is a gift of the Spirit. Challenges are faced when the good news crosses language and cultural barriers, as demonstrated by the cultural-translation issues faced by Paul and Barnabas in Lystra (Acts 14:11-14), but the fact that even these challenges are recorded in Scripture only confirms God's intention to make His Word known in every language and culture. John's grand vision at the end of the Bible reveals that Jesus is Lord over all languages and cultures. The Lamb has purchased people from every culture and language (Revelation 5:9). A multitude from every

---

[9] The Greek translation of the Old Testament is called the *Septuagint* (LXX).

culture and language will worship Him and proclaim the good news of salvation (Revelation 7:9).

The good news of Jesus is translatable across cultures, and the history of the spread of Christianity from the first century until today bears witness to the diverse languages and cultures the gospel has crossed to make its way to us. To think that Christianity is a Western religion is to be both ignorant of history and the current state of the church. Visit a Christian churches in South Korea, India, Nigeria, Brazil, and Singapore, and you will only begin to get a taste of the cultural and linguistic diversity of the global church today. The language and worship in each of these churches will be distinct, though the Spirit is the same. The one Word of God is being proclaimed and worshipped across different languages and cultures. The gospel being proclaimed in these churches is one gospel, translated into a multitude of languages and cultural expressions. Each of these languages and cultures is on the move and continuing to change, and yet the ancient text of the Bible is impacting the diverse cultural forms and languages across Asia, Africa, and South America. The Bible is able to handle the continual cultural transformation and change, because God intended for His Word to be translatable.

We need not worry whether the ancient text of the Bible can be translated into the culture of today's youth. The ancient text of Scripture impacted the young Goth warriors when Ulfilas translated the Bible in the third century, just as much as the ancient text of the Bible impacted the Huaorani people as Rachel Saint risked all to cross that distant language and culture barrier.[10] If the Bible has already been proven to grasp the hearts in such a diversity of cultures before, the difference between Gen X, Gen Z, and the upcoming Gen Alpha is not so large of a chasm. The Word will be translated and planted into the next generation.

---

[10] Steve Saint, *End of the Spear: A True Story* (Carol Stream, Ill: Tyndale House Publishers, 2005).

Whether in crossing geographic cultures or generational cultures, the translation principle functions similarly. Because culture is always moving and flowing, there are language and cultural differences between generations, and so the Bible must be re-translated into the language and cultural forms of the generation into which the kingdom is expanding. The Ancient Text is as relevant to the next generation as it was to the previous one. When we communicate with people of our own language and culture, then we can communicate using the language and cultural forms that make sense to us. When we go abroad and speak with people in another distant culture, it is obvious that we must use their language and cultural forms. Perhaps the biggest challenge is when we plant the Word of God into a culture that is very much like ours, and yet has changed in significant but less perceptible ways. In this case, the need for translation may not be as obvious to us, but as the cultural flow moves further and further downstream, the differences eventually become large enough that we do need a new translation. We need to entrust the proclamation of the gospel to someone who is embedded within that cultural current.

How does God plant the ancient word of the Bible into cultural flows? When Jesus taught about the kingdom of God, His parables would compare the idea of a seed with the Word of God. Jesus' teaching helps us to understand how we are to plant the gospel of the Ancient Text into an ever-changing culture. The sower scatters the seed onto the soil and four types of soil receive it differently. If we want the Word of the Ancient Text to bear fruit, we must first receive it into our life. We cannot close our ears to it, let the things of life choke it out, or receive it with only a shallow welcome, but we must let the seed sink deep into us, and let the Word take root in our lives. When we accept and receive the life-changing Word, anchoring our faith to the Scripture, it will produce fruit in the cultures around us and those that we have contact with. We cannot abstract the text from within our own langua-cultural flow. It is already here and available, and so we only need to read it, accept it, not let it be choked out by distractions, and let it take deep root and bear abundant fruit in our lives (Mark 4:1-20). The seed itself will do the work. Just like a farmer who scatters the seed, once we plant it in our life, in our cultural linguistic flow, it will take root and grow into a harvest (Mark 4:26-29). It seems small. Can the ancient text of the Bible really have that much impact? When God's Word is sown in our cultural soil, it begins small, but the great tree of the kingdom of God will sprout out of this seed (Mark 4:30-32).

In the gospel of John, Jesus also spoke of how the kingdom of Heaven will come through a seed. Jesus said that unless a seed falls to the ground and dies, it remains by itself. "But if it dies, it produces much fruit" (John 12:24). Jesus is the Word of God and He is the seed who died, was buried, and rose up to so that His Word can be planted among all nations, languages, and cultures. But here Jesus also sets a pattern for us. When we teach the Bible to other cultures, whether far cultures or even to people of the same culture who are slightly further down the stream of culture change, we must plant a seed that dies. If we try to maintain the life of our own culture and plant the seed of the Bible by championing our own culture and privileging our own language, our seed will remain by itself. We must join Jesus, empty ourselves of the cultural forms we hold so dear, and allow them to die. God's eternal Word will sprout in new cultural forms, and new languages, with different terms and worship styles, but it is the same seed and the same Spirit. As the river of life flows from Jerusalem to the nations, it is not producing one tree with one fruit, but an abundant variety and diversity of trees with leaves for the healing of all nations. There will be a multitude of varieties of fish and all kinds of trees (Ezekiel 47:9-12). This was Ezekiel's vision, and it is as certain as any word in Scripture!

God's Word is eternal. The changing cultural currents that have been twisting throughout our globe over the past two thousand years have not drowned His Word. The ancient psalmist's poem on Scripture can act as fertilizer for our soil. Psalm 119 reminds us that we must treasure His Word. We must obey His Word. We must put our faith and trust in His Word. We must meditate on His Word, set His Word before us, and cling to it. When I was a year old, my parents put me in a baby backpack and took me walking out onto a coral reef, and a small tsunami came crashing in toward them. My parents clung onto the rock wall, and I held on to my dad's neck with all my baby-like strength.[11] I was secure. My father held me. We have a much surer rock to hold onto when the cultural waves crash around us and into us. We have to cling to the rock of Scripture, as it will never fail.

Culture and language are human forms and change as humans change. We must be vigilant to not let go of Scripture, but we can have complete confidence that the Scripture we have is God's Word. The Incarnate Word affirms the written Word of God. Jesus is risen and the Holy Spirit is active. Scripture is not at the mercy of our changing cultural tides, but God will be faithful to preserve His Word. He has been through all the changes until now, though there have been struggles to be sure, we can have confidence in His Word among the multitude of cultural flows today. Our faith in Scripture is an anchor and can allow us to not be set adrift in our changing culture. However, we must be willing to die to ourselves and allow the seed of the Word of God to be planted in the cultural-linguistic current that is downstream. We can entrust the Ancient Text to be translated and re-expressed afresh. Youth today are the cultural translators taking the Word downstream on the cultural current and wave. Perhaps we can't ride that wave, but they can. We can know that the seed of God's ancient and eternal Word will sprout to an abundant harvest in every culture and language yet to come.

---

[11] I, of course, do not remember this episode. But have heard it many times as my parents shared with me the fear in that moment!

CHAPTER 9

MODERN SCHOOLS AND AN ANCIENT TEXT

Dondi E. Costin, Ph.D.

The most enduring takeaway from the driver's education course I endured the summer before my 16th birthday goes like this: *there is no such thing as a safe intersection.* As couplets go, *dangerous intersection* is as redundant as *safe intersection* is oxymoronic, and this timely reminder has saved my bacon from behind the wheel on multiple continents for more than 40 years. I have Coach Joe Miller to thank for that life lesson.

Coach Miller knew the laws of physics are tough teachers, so he was even tougher on us to ensure we learned from him that summer rather than from them down the road. Safety requires being aware of your surroundings, keeping your head on a swivel, respecting the potential for collision, and driving defensively all the way through the intersection so you can reach your destination. Longevity requires repeating that process at every single intersection because you never know when the other guy might confuse a roadway for a speedway. This kind of defensive driving is what it means to be *street smart*. Wise as a serpent, harmless as a dove.

The same is true regarding the potential for collision at the intersection of modern schools and the Ancient Text, only the stakes are far higher when worldviews clash than when cars crash. We teach an Ancient Text that never changes and is always sure (Isaiah 40:8), but we teach this text in a modern context that features the kind of paganism that marked the culture in which the text first spoke.[1] This rivalry makes for the most dangerous of intersections among those whose driving passions include both our Ancient Text and the students who populate our modern schools. Since road rage is on the rise, *street smarts* are especially wise.

A World Gone Mad

Every generation has declared at some point that their culture has finally hit rock bottom. Each has decried the sense that the good old days are long gone and only the Dark Ages remain. We can lay some of that perception at the feet of our own inner curmudgeon, and something tells me that every language has its own way of saying, *"Get off my lawn!"* But when modern lovers of the Ancient Text echo those sentiments, they bring data to make their case.

Evidence for our deep concern turns up everywhere. It appears that Western culture has been *dechristianized* by stripping the biblical worldview from the policy conversation and *dehumanized* by sidelining God's plan for human flourishing from polite conversation.[2] The devaluing of human life in the womb, abandoning of biblical sexual mores, the collapse of marriage, fractured families, gender confusion, racial strife, undercutting of religious liberty,[3] and a dramatically increasing mental health crisis[4] narrate this tale

---

[1] Steven D. Smith, *Pagans and Christians in the City: Culture Wars from the Tiber to the Potomac* (Grand Rapids, MI: William B. Eerdmans Publishing Company, 2018).

[2] R. Albert Mohler, *The Gathering Storm: Secularism, Culture, and the Church* (Nashville TN: Nelson Books, 2020), 189-190.

[3] David Platt, *Counter Culture: Following Christ in an Anti-Christian Age* (Carol Stream, IL: Tyndale Momentum, 2017).

[4] Mental Health America, "2021 State of Mental Health in America," accessed May 22, 2022, https://mhanational.org/research-reports/2021-state-mental-health-america.

of woe. Considering that 74 percent of American millennials believe that "whatever is right for your life or works best for you is the only truth you can know,"[5] there is little wonder that we now live in a world gone mad.

A slate of contemporary writers traces this madness to incremental shifts away from God across successive generations, culminating in what Carl Trueman has so carefully documented as *The Rise and Triumph of the Modern Self*.[6] This modern self is increasingly triumphant in displays of "expressive individualism" that would be unrecognizable even to the vaunted "Me" generation of days gone by. In a concise restatement of his landmark work aimed at a more general audience, Trueman calls his more popular book *Strange New World*.[7] This new world is the context in which modern schools and our Ancient Text find themselves on a collision course.

As much as we want to believe that Christian students are in this world but not of it (1 John 2:15-17), the saturating influence of social and other popular media indicate that the prevailing winds are against us. Our culture appears bound to a set of principles that directly counter the narrative we find in the Ancient Text. Mark Clark succinctly summarizes five radical cultural shifts maddening our world as we speak:

1. Individual happiness and personal freedom are now the highest goods.

2. Anything that limits happiness or self-expression must be destroyed.

3. Technology and education will lead to enlightenment, so we do not need God.

4. Feelings trump facts. Objective truth does not exist. *My truth is all that matters.*

---

[5] Tara Isabella Burton, *Strange Rites: New Religions for a Godless World* (New York: Public Affairs, 2020), 164.

[6] Carl R. Trueman, *The Rise and Triumph of the Modern Self: Cultural Amnesia, Expressive Individualism, and the Road to Sexual Revolution* (Wheaton, IL: Crossway, 2020).

[7] Carl R. Trueman, *Strange New World: How Thinkers and Activists Redefined Identity and Sparked the Sexual Revolution* (Wheaton, IL: Crossway, 2022).

5. Personal authenticity trumps external authority, so institutions like the church are worth my time only when they advance my version of self-fulfillment. Everyone believes in something, but the God of the Bible is just one of many viable options.[8]

Undoubtedly, the students in our classrooms are steeping in a modern mindset that conflicts with Scripture at every turn. Author Tara Burton articulates how these modern sensibilities might sound if we could read aloud our prospective students' minds:

> I am the only truth I know. My emotions are God-given. They tell me what to do and how to live. To be my truest self I should follow my instincts. My body and my gut know more than my mind. An unjust and repressive society has held me back from becoming my best self. It has warped my faith in my own abilities and my relationships with others. I owe it to myself to practice self-care. I owe it to the world to perfect myself: physically, spiritually, morally. There is no objective right or wrong. Different people and different societies have different moral obligations.[9]

Hauntingly, Burton suggests this narrative has effectively become a rival religion for an "intuitional culture" in hot pursuit of meaning, purpose, ritual, and community.[10] We know that no individual or organization offers a better answer for these fundamental concerns than Jesus Christ and His Church, so we clearly have work to do through the vehicle of our modern schools.

Since the Ancient Text opposes modernity in every meaningful sense, our current traffic situation is an accident waiting to happen. In fact, we now stand at the crash scene. When joined to the sad reality that the Ancient Text, its Author, and its adherents are in-

---

[8] Mark Clark, "5 Cultural Shifts We Must Understand to Reach Our Neighbors," 14 June, 2021, accessed May 21, 2022, https://outreachmagazine.com/ features/evangelism/67237-5-cultural-shifts-we-must-understand-to-reach-our-neighbors.

[9] Burton, 165.

[10] Burton, 166.

creasingly viewed as out-of-touch, old-school radicals bent on spoiling the party for everyone else, someone should dial 911.

Back to the Future

In this emergency, however, we should start by dialing what believers have often referred to as God's phone number. When all else fails, He never does, and there is no time like the present. Jeremiah 33:2-3 reminds us that desperate times call for desperate measures: "This is what the LORD says, he who made the earth, the LORD who formed it and established it—the LORD is his name: 'Call to me and I will answer you and tell you great and unsearchable things you do not know.'" (NIV). Leaders of modern schools would almost universally agree that these are desperate times. Fortunately, God knows this road like the back of His hand.

There is great confidence in knowing that the Lord has accomplished His purposes through His people in every century and in every culture, whether or not those centuries and cultures have been friendly to His people or His cause. Beginning with Adam and Eve, the currents of modern thought have persistently pushed people to unseat God by assuming their ways are better than his ways despite clear evidence to the contrary (Isaiah 55:8-9). Almost from day one, humans have entertained Satan's vexing interrogatory—"*Did God really say?*"—as a prelude to questioning for themselves God's wisdom and His ways. Without exception, believing Satan's lie—"*You will not surely die*"—leads to distracted driving on life's highway, the end of which is death (Genesis 3).

Rather than submit to God and the external authorities He has established for our good (Proverbs 3:5-6), we consistently chart our own course instead—always to our detriment. It is no coincidence that travelers often describe their condition as lost. This destructive pattern is repeated across the millennia with predictable results. As Scripture makes abundantly clear, "each person is tempted when they are dragged away by their own evil desire and enticed. Then, after desire has conceived, it gives birth to sin; and sin, when it is full-grown, gives birth to death" (James 1:14-15, NIV). In every direction, as far as the eye can see, we have instinctively followed our ancestors' lead in doing what is right in our own eyes (Judges 21:25).

As the apostle Paul's Roman audience learned the hard way, Shakespeare's "to thine own self be true" only works when thine own self is fully aligned with God. Absent that solid ground, sheer madness ensues. Perhaps no single morsel of the Ancient Text is more striking, forceful, and relevant to the challenges facing our modern schools than these inspired words from Paul's pen:

> The wrath of God is being revealed from heaven against all the godlessness and wickedness of people, who suppress the truth by their wickedness, since what may be known about God is plain to them, because God has made it plain to them. ... so that people are without excuse.
>
> For although they knew God, they neither glorified him as God nor gave thanks to him, but their thinking became futile and their foolish hearts were darkened. Although they claimed to be wise, they became fools and exchanged the glory of the immortal God for images made to look like a mortal human being and birds and animals and reptiles. Therefore, God gave them over in the sinful desires of their hearts to sexual impurity for the degrading of their bodies with one another. They exchanged the truth about God for a lie, and worshipped and served created things rather than the Creator....
>
> Because of this, God gave them over to shameful lusts. Even their women exchanged natural sexual relations for unnatural ones. In the same way the men also abandoned natural relations with women and were inflamed with lust for one another. Men committed shameful acts with other men, and received in themselves the due penalty for their error.
>
> Furthermore, since they did not think it worthwhile to retain the knowledge of God, so God gave them over to a depraved mind, so that they do what ought not to be done. They have

become filled with every kind of wickedness, evil, greed and depravity. They are full of envy, murder, strife, deceit, and malice. They are gossips, slanderers, God-haters, insolent, arrogant and boastful; they invent ways of doing evil; they disobey their parents; they have no understanding, no fidelity, no love, no mercy. Although they know God's righteous decree that those who do such things deserve death, they not only continue to do these very things but also approve of those who practice them (Romans 1:18-32, NIV).

Despite (and perhaps because of) our numerous technological and other innovations, digesting Paul's analysis of his culture takes me back to the future. Or, in the words of the immortal Yogi Berra, the Ancient Text gives the sense of "déjà vu all over again."

It is striking that so many of Paul's cultural characterizations in Romans 1 relate directly to the role schools should play in advancing the gospel today. Countering the following cultural maladies of head and heart with biblical solutions is right in our wheelhouse:

"Suppress the truth by their wickedness" (verse 18);

"What may be known about God is plain to them" (verse 19);

"Their thinking became futile and their foolish hearts were darkened" (verse 21);

"Although they claimed to be wise, they became fools" (verse 22);

"They exchanged the truth about God for a lie" (verse 25);

"They did not think it worthwhile to retain the knowledge of God;" and

"God gave them over to a depraved mind" (verse 28) (NIV).

One preacher's proverb encourages us to keep the Bible in one hand and the newspaper in the other. Being true to the Ancient Text requires us to read today's newspaper through the Bible's lens, of course, not the other way around. This is precisely what Paul had in mind as he wrote to his friends in Rome, who found themselves immersed in a culture that sounds a lot like ours.

Christ Makes the Difference

Paul's response to the modern problem, fixed at the dangerous intersection to which God had assigned him, was to point his culture to the glories of Christ. Following his argument, a few verses into the second chapter of Romans brings us to this preliminary conclusion, which serves as a fitting summary of the gospel solution we have been commanded to share: "To those who by persistence in doing good seek glory, honor, and immortality, he will give eternal life. But for those who are self-seeking and who reject the truth and follow evil, there will be wrath and anger" (Romans 2:7-8, NIV). We Christians understand that the good Paul commends is not at salvation's root but is its fruit. We also understand that our "persistence in doing good" should consist of helping "those who are self-seeking and who reject the truth" to follow Christ instead. In short, modern schools help modern selves embrace the mind of Christ (1 Corinthians 2:16).

Similar to Paul, for Christ "and his name's sake, we received grace and apostleship to call people from among all the Gentiles to the obedience that comes from faith" (Romans 1:5). While none among us can be apostles in the foundational way Paul could make that claim, leaders of modern schools find themselves directing traffic in the most dangerous of intersections using the Ancient Text to transport self-seeking, truth-rejecting, expressive individualists from death to life. Like the apostle, we are "obligated both to Greeks and non-Greeks, both to the wise and the foolish ... to preach the gospel." We, too, must not be "ashamed of the gospel, because it is the power of God that brings salvation to everyone who believes" (Romans 1:14-16, NIV).

Like any effective leader, Paul practiced what he preached. In Thessalonica he "reasoned with them from the Scriptures" (Acts 17:2, NIV). In Berea he made a mad dash to the synagogue, where "they received the message with great eagerness and examined the Scriptures every day to see if what Paul said was true. As a result, many of them believed" (Acts 17:11b-12a). In Athens "he was greatly distressed to see that the city was full of idols. So, he reasoned in the synagogue with both Jews and God-fearing Greeks, as well as in the marketplace day by day with those who happened to be there" (Acts 17:16-17, NIV). Not to be outdone by the academics in Athens, he debated both Epicurean and Stoic philosophers who were so intrigued with his "strange ideas" that they asked him to address a larger meeting of the Areopagus to help them make sense of it all (Acts 17:18-21). He used that platform to cross the intersection of modern thinking and the Ancient Text for the sake of the gospel. And as is often the case, "some of them sneered, but others" wanted to hear more (Acts 17:22-32). Regardless of results, our calling is the same.

Go and Teach

Our calling is actually a commission straight from the lips of Jesus, whose parting shot decimated all uncertainty regarding his plans for his people until his return. That plan is to teach.

> Then the eleven disciples went to Galilee, to the mountain where Jesus had told them to go. When they saw him, they worshipped him; but some doubted. Then Jesus came to them and said, "All authority in heaven and on earth has been given to me. Therefore go and make disciples of nations, baptizing them in the name of the Father and of the Son and of the Holy Spirit, and teaching them to obey everything I have commanded you. And surely, I am with you always, to the very end of the age (Matthew 28:16-20, NIV).

It is hard to imagine a commission more clarifying and comforting than this one. No wonder they call it Great.

For starters, I am drawn to the presence of doubters in the crowd. They comfort me because Scripture calls them disciples (learners), yet their doubt does not affect the Commission Jesus gave them. These disciples had plenty of reason to doubt, especially since their prospect pool opposed their message in every significant way—culturally, socially, theologically, and politically. Jesus acknowledged their doubt, understood it completely, but commissioned them anyway because there is no other plan. His authority as the basis for our life's work multiplies our comfort. Most comforting of all is His promise to be with us through every inch of the intersection. No seatbelt could ever hope to match the security of the Savior.

Finally, modern school educators must not miss the Commission's climactic flourish. Sandwiched between His God-given authority and the promise of His presence, Jesus commands His disciples to make more disciples. Teaching is ultimate in this arrangement, the end of which is equipping others "to obey everything I have commanded you" (Matthew 28:20). In this instance more than any other, learning is for living.

The saints of old remind us that the safest place for anyone is the center of God's will. That only happens when the Spirit of God applies His Ancient Text to hearts and minds. In an increasingly secular society, modern schools must drive through this intersection like they own the place, or, better yet, like they know the One who does. Led by those with the heart of a teacher and the mind of Christ, even the most expressive individualist can, "in view of God's mercy," learn "to offer [their] bodies as living sacrifices, holy and pleasing to God." No longer conforming "to the pattern of this world," they can "be transformed by the renewing of [their] mind. Then [they] will be able to test and approve what God's will is—his good, pleasing and perfect will" (Romans 12:1-2, NIV). They can then be sure to get home in one piece.

SECTION III

EDUCATION AND MINISTRY TO A MODERN STUDENT

Another key component in gardening is the work of the gardener. As I look at students today, one of my main questions is "Where are the gardeners?" Our students more than ever need a team of gardeners in their lives. Research continues to show that one of the most important correlations with faith maturity in students today is the number of adults who are invested in students' spiritual journeys. If you are reading this book, you most likely are a gardener in a student's life. This section will help us to be good gardeners that apply the Ancient Text into ministry and Christian education of a modern student. It will help us to think through the framework of building a student ministry based on the Word of God, utilizing a team of caring adults, that disciples modern students and produces spiritual fruit.

CHAPTER 10

HOW TO REACH THIS GENERATION

Jay H. Strack, D.Min.

Whoever wants the next generation will win them. Years ago I was privileged to be conducting a crusade in Albany, Georgia. The lead church in this county-wide outreach was Dr. Michael Catt of Sherwood Baptist Church. Walking through the foyer, I saw that on a banner and immediately hung it on the wall of my heart. It has become one of the main motivational quotes of my life.

This dynamic church took reaching and keeping this generation seriously, and this moment instilled in me the real understanding that nothing happens apart from a partnership with a strong, Great Commission-minded, committed local church. Dr. Catt became a catalyst for the call on my life to found Student Leadership University and some 280,000 students and youth ministry leaders have been resourced, trained, and inspired as a result. Whoever puts the most effort into leading this generation will win their hearts and minds. Whether it is alcohol or drug industries, media signals and messages, cults, or the cultural warriors, Satan may not be permitted to have this generation; not on my watch. In this chapter, I share the insights I have learned over 40 years of ministry. Together, let us train this generation to influence the next for the Kingdom. Psalm 78:4 charges us with this:

"We will not hide these truths from our children;

we will tell the next generation

about the glorious deeds of the LORD,

about his power and his mighty wonders."[1]

Let's be honest and up front. As hard as we all try, youth leaders are often overwhelmed with the enormity of the needs and the day-to-day grind of student ministry. After training thousands of youth ministers, I still see many who are trying their hardest but don't know how to get from where they are to where they want to go. Whether its Google, YouTube, Siri, or other media outlets, there is a plethora of ideas to be found online. Obviously, we do not lack information. We lack insight.

As I have the opportunity to speak to aspiring leaders who desire to be used by God, I always begin with sharing three core insights I learned from the front lines of youth ministry.

1. No generation has ever been *easy* to reach so do not be overwhelmed with this one.

2. Only the truths of the Scriptures are worth building your life on, and we must enable students to transfer these truths as their own system of belief.

3. Spiritual leaders are needed now, today, and across the world.

I thank you for joining me in this chapter, but I want to ask you to decide now to finish what you start.

According to an article in the New York Times, only 36% of Americans complete a nonfiction e-book.[2] It's easier to start something new than to finish what makes you think, prioritize, and consider

---

[1] *Holy Bible*, New Living Translation, copyright © 1996, 2004, 2015 by Tyndale House Foundation. Used by permission of Tyndale House Publishers, Inc., Carol Stream, Illinois 60188. All rights reserved.

[2] *Keeping Tabs on Best-Seller Books and Reading Habits*. (n.d.). Retrieved July 15, 2022, from https://www.newyorktimes.com.

change. WARNING: Don't be content to check into a digital screen throughout most of the day, snatching bits of insight. I challenge you to grab a pen, pencil, lipstick, or mascara to underline all parts of this book that the Holy Spirit highlights in your mind.

Overview of the Generations[3]

Generations	Years Born	Age Now (2023)
Gen A or Alpha Gen	2012–2025	0–11
Gen Z	1997–2012	11–26
Gen Y or Millennials	1981–1996	27 – 42
Gen X	1965–1980	43–58
Boomers	1946–1964	59–77

Each generation must deal with the battle for the mind, the battle for the body, the mind, the soul, and their future. They might look different as to fashion choices, haircuts, the music they like, or the language they use to communicate, but the internal battle for the next generation has always been the same.

While the conversations in ministry meetings may center around staying on the cutting edge of technology, I have seen over decades that the more high-tech society becomes, the more high-touch we need to be in meeting needs, listening, and embodying compassion. Students don't care how much you know until they know how much you care. There is no expiration date for this observation.

Signature Insight One – No Generation Has Ever Been *Easy* to Reach

At 16, I was a meth addict. Drugs and alcohol helped me numb the pain of broken homes, no dad in my life, abuse, and no sense of purpose. Salvation in Jesus came to me through the Jesus Move-

---

[3] *Boomers, Gen X, Gen Y, Gen Z, and Gen A explained.* (n.d.). Kasasa. Retrieved July 15, 2022, from https://www.kasasa.com/exchange/articles/generations/gen-x-gen-y-gen-z.

ment, arguably the last great revival movement in the United States. Since the age of 17, my great privilege has been to strive to reach this generation with the gospel.

I have spoken in more than 10,000 high schools over the years. In the 70s the issues most requested by educators were:

- Evolution
- Safe Sex
- Drugs and Alcohol

In the 80s and 90s another issue came out of the closet.

- Gay Pride

As a pastor at the time, I felt the hatred from both sides. People wanted to understand the AIDS epidemic—Was it a sin? Was it God's punishment? I spoke out with compassion but did not (and never will) change my biblical worldview. As a result, my home was vandalized. And what began as a movement to "come out of the closet" is now publicly and proudly proclaimed in parades and events across screens worldwide. "For if the trumpet makes an uncertain sound, who will prepare for battle?" (1 Corinthians 14:8, NKJV).

Recently, I heard someone use the words "New Normal" in a news report of a crime. I thought about that phrase and realized that it is now a tragically correct description of many behaviors and issues this generation faces. The acceptance of immoral behavior has become more public in discussion and normal in acceptance.

I recently had a roundtable of diverse college students in my home to discuss what they are facing and how we can address these issues from a biblical worldview perspective. These were the top three they wanted to discuss:

- Transgenderism
- Mental Health
- How do you know what is truth?

Understandably, students are confused about what is true, what is right, when all around them mixed messages fill the air. A search on Google for the word *rumor* brought up 972,000,000 websites in .71 seconds; a search for the word *truth* found 3,010,000,000 sites in .65 seconds.[4]

These are serious issues with sub-issues and baggage to match, but they are not reasons to give up on reaching this generation. If you are going to be a key player in the lives of students, this information should inspire you to work hard, listen longer, and teach through the Word of God as an anointed, called-out servant of Christ.

My good friend Josh McDowell recently wrote in his latest book *Free to Thrive,* "Medical and mental health professionals confirm that much of the dysfunction and disconnectedness we experience in life stems from unresolved relational and emotional hurts. These hurts leave us with unfulfilled God-given longings that we seek to fulfill through unhealthy behaviors and relationships."[5]

He lists the seven longings that need to be met for a life of fulfillment as:

- acceptance
- appreciation
- affection
- access
- attention
- affirmation of feelings
- assurance of safety

Every generation lives with unmet longings that can only be met by Jesus and the truth of His Word. If you are going to reach this generation, look beyond the behaviors and get to the heart of the

---

[4] *Google.* (n.d.-b). www.google.com. Retrieved July 15, 2022, from http://www.google.com.
[5] McDowell, J., Bennett, B., & Cloud, H. (2021). Excerpt from back book cover, *Free to Thrive: How Your Hurt, Struggles, and Deepest Longings Can Lead to a Fulfilling Life.* Thomas Nelson.

matter. Remember, "Jesus Christ is the same yesterday, today, and forever" (Hebrews 13:8, NKJV).

Signature Insight Two – The Bible Is THE Book to Build Your Life On

The Billy Graham Training Center at The Cove shared this in a 2012 blog post:

> We do have a code book. We do have a key. We do have authoritative source material. It is found in the ancient and historic Book we call the Bible. This Book has come down to us through the ages. It has passed through so many hands, appeared in so many forms—and survived attack of every kind. Neither barbaric vandalism nor civilized scholarship has touched it. Neither the burning of fire nor the laughter of skepticism has accomplished its annihilation. Through the many dark ages of man its glorious promises have survived unchanged."[6]

Just a few minutes of watching a news channel will confirm:

- There never has been a time when the Bible is more relevant and needed than it is today.

- There has never been a time when the Bible has been more neglected, even by people who claim to follow Jesus.

Author and famed Texas Pastor George W. Truitt once preached, "There is no failure in God's will, and no success outside of God's will."[7] After these decades of training thousands of leaders and students in biblical worldview, I am more convinced that the most important step in any life is to build a life on the truth, wisdom, and will of God as revealed in the Scriptures. Where each generation

---

[6] *The Need for Wisdom*. (11 May, 2013). Billy Graham Training Center at the Cove. Retrieved from https://thecove.org/blog/devotion/the-need-for-wisdom/.

[7] George W. Truett Quotes. Retrieved from https://quotefancy.com/george-w-truett-quotes.

rises or falls is on choosing God's Word or the words of friends, peers, intimidation, and culture.

The history books of both church and modern history are full of the biographies of those who successfully conquered the worst of times by building life unapologetically on God's Word. Within the same pages are the notes of those who gave in to seek fame, fortune, and popularity as life's priority. These were left searching for more.

One thought permeated my mind as the idea for founding Student Leadership University circled me daily. How could I help these students find ownership of the truths of God's Word? It isn't enough to say "I learned it at church. My mom and dad said it's true." They must first know the truth of God's Word; and second, they need to believe it as their own. Only then can they make life's most important decisions instead of being swept into the noise of the culture.

I am fascinated by the book *Making the Mummies Dance* by author Thomas Hoving, Ph.D. Hoving became a legend for the clandestine deals that secured blockbuster exhibitions for the Metropolitan Museum of Art. The stories were amazing, but it was the title that stuck with me. How do we make the Word of God "dance" for students so that they understand its significance and are in awe of its magnificence?

When I take students to Israel through our SLU 401 program, I teach them to hold historical proofs of the Bible's veracity in their minds. The grand narrative of the Bible explains all other stories. These, I promise them, will defeat the giants of doubt, discouragement, despair, and disillusion. I understand that students are not always excited about learning biblical history, but we do have to interject facts that support the veracity of God's Word "so the next generation would know them, even the children yet to be born, and they in turn would tell their children" (Psalm 78:6, NIV).

Signature Insight Three—Spiritual Leaders Are Needed Now

"To be the man you have to beat the man" – Ric Flair

The first sentence out of my mouth at an SLU 101 event is, "There has to be a time in every life when a little boy sits down, and a young man stands up. And there has to be a time when a little girl sits down, and a young woman stands up." That is the moment a student accepts the responsibility to lead and takes ownership of the choices that will make define his or her future. History books are not filled with stories of the average person. They detail stories of the great—those who courageously battled the odds and won. Every youth leader must make it their goal to help students understand the strength and influence that comes from a faithful life. That is the beginning of leadership.

Can we lead in a modern world that is completely opposed to what we believe? We can, and we can do it successfully and powerfully.

Leadership Is Influence

First, understand that leadership is not a title or a position. It's not a rank. To be a servant leader is to follow the example lived out by the Lord Jesus. He led daily and they followed, but His leadership began with serving. We follow His footprints as we serve; we follow His fingerprints as we live by a biblical worldview. Remember: this is more caught than it is taught.

The word *leadership* has been thrown around by marketers, corporations, and multitudes of books. Three decades ago, I began to study the leadership principles of my friend, John Maxwell, and continually read almost every book he has authored. Twenty-five years ago, as Student Leadership University was just taking off, John stopped by my office for lunch. I asked the question, "With all the discussions on leadership, how do you define it?" John wrote on a napkin that day, "Leadership is influence." I still teach it every week in our programs.

Influence is privilege, and one we must be thoughtful in. As a leader, our decisions, our words, and our choices influence those students who watch and listen to us, even when we are not aware. Many leaders have lost their influence because of one bad choice. All the work you put in can be quickly forgotten as students and others process your double standard. Be aware that these temptations can and will happen to anyone, no matter how many times you quote the disciple Peter by saying, "Never Lord!"

On a mission trip at the age of 19, I looked up in awe to the missions' pastors who had invited me. When they said, "Jay, you need to cut your long hair. You cannot be a witness to Jesus. Go and pray about it." I left and went to my room, but later as I went to their room to talk, I saw them come in with women from that foreign land. Anyone can fall when they think no one is looking. But believe it—Jesus is always looking. And you should be always looking at what your future will be.

Many years ago, I was traveling way too much away from my family. I was exhausted, lonely, and stressed over needed finances to cover the crusades and staff we had taken on. Women often came up to shake my hand after the services and some held on a little too long, but this time I got a phone call in my room. I knew who she was for she had come to the crusade every night, sitting near the front row, and afterward came up to speak with me. "I am in the lobby," she said. "Can you come down to meet with me or should I come up?" I will be honest and tell you that I fought with that demon for a minute, but the Holy Spirit instantly called me to Himself, and I won the battle. The questions before me were, "Jay do you love your wife, Diane? Do you love your daughters? Do you love me?" The struggle was not that I wasn't committed to Christ or didn't want to serve Him. Not because I didn't love my wife. But because I had allowed myself to be vulnerable.

This situation also made me desire accountability. My faithful directors on my ministry's board have become my closest friends, asking me questions regularly. I honestly share struggles and prayer needs. I submit to this willfully and even joyfully for I want nothing to move me away from my personal call to follow Christ. One of the greatest decisions you can make in life and ministry is to see a godly, trustworthy accountability partner and prayer warriors who will join you in the daily fight against the evil one.

Future-tense thinkers make decisions that lead to a life of a faithful legacy. If we are going to live faithfully and lead well in this modern world, we must take our cues from the Word of God. Here are my key components of spiritual leadership:

Leaders Make Things Better

I can see the wheels spinning in your head. You might suffer from what many call *the imposter syndrome.* You might be saying "I'm not sure that I am able to be an influencer." This is not true. Anyone can earn the right to lead by serving others. It is a daily mindset that says, "I want to make things better."

My good friend Dr. David Ferguson has a D.Phil. from Oxford. The man is brilliant, but people know him as a servant leader who is always ready to listen. David and I have been friends for decades, serving together in foreign countries and teaching in conferences across the land. One day he sat next to me and said, "Jay Strack, I have you figured out." I was intrigued because I have never figured myself out! He said, "You look at a situation that most people walk away from and say, 'That is not right. It shouldn't be.' And then you sit down and begin to minister to that person and say, 'How do we fix this?'" This philosopher factored in my life of abuse and learning at an early age to protect my mom and myself and figured out my way of thinking. And, I have to say, he is right.

Leaders Make Things Better by Listening Before They Talk.

I am a big believer that when everyone else walks away, we should pull up a chair and listen. Understand I am not saying we condone behavior or cast our judgment in that moment. But we do pull up a chair and show unconditional love. It is often difficult to get your mind around a strange situation, but we must because in this world we will face many unanswered questions and many disappointments.

To be an effective leader, you have to start where you are and not from where you wish you were. Please get this: Leadership is not about you being in charge. It's not about being "the one" everyone comes to or having your name listed first.

Many years ago, I spoke at a chapel for players before the NBA All-Star Game at Madison Square Garden. In those days, each team was permitted to send one member to the All-Star game. Knowing this, I spoke on Shamgar and the power of one (Judges 3:31). When you do as Shamgar did, you start where you are, do what you can, and use what you have. As we read, it works. Don't get hung up on the ministries that have more funds, more people, more exposure than you do.

My first youth group was seven teens I gathered from speaking at a local public school. None of them had a religious background, but they did like pizza. When the invite included free pizza and the chance to talk about "what do you want to do with your life?" they spread the word and we outgrew the meeting spot quickly. *Wherever God has placed you, settle in and work hard.* He can do more with less if a heart is willing to trust. We get so hung up on what we don't have that we forget Who has us!

Believe with all your heart that "God can do anything, you know—far more than you could ever imagine or guess or request in your wildest dreams! He does it not by pushing us around but by working within us, his Spirit deeply and gently within us" (Ephesians 3:20, MSG).[8]

You can make a difference in your generation, your family, your school, and your city if you simply start where you are and lead people to God's unlimited agenda instead of your limited one. In my life, I am in a lot of meetings, far more than I want to be. Sometimes, I'm the guy in charge. The meeting starts when I get there, and it stops when I go. On other days, I am one of the team, listening and learning. I call that the opportunity to hang out with eagles, one of my favorite things to do. Often, I am the guy gathering extra chairs, handing out notebooks, and getting a chance to shake a hand or make someone laugh.

Let me give you an example of servant leadership that I experienced recently. My friend, John Maxwell, who I mentioned earlier, flew in from an event in Las Vegas where he saw several thousand come to Christ publicly. It was a secular, corporate event of 50,000 people and he invited at the end, "Hey, I am staying over if you want to come worship with me tomorrow morning." They responded to his invitation because he led them well and thousands came to Christ. The next night he flew into Charleston to speak at a *Mega Metro Pastors Conference* of about 70 people. I called and said, "John, you are off tonight, and I know you are tired. Do you want to just have dinner and go to your room?" He answered, "No, I would like to go to the conference dinner and talk to the pastors and listen to the message." He did just that. No ego over the thousands he had just spoken to or what God had done; only the thought of building relationships and caring about pastors. That is a servant leader of the most effective kind.

Leaders Have to Lead Themselves

You will never be a leader of others if you cannot lead yourself. You cannot motivate anyone if you are not motivated. You cannot

---

[8] *The Message* (MSG). Copyright © 1993, 2002, 2018 by Eugene H. Peterson.

talk about servant leadership if you don't have a servant's heart. Showing up, doing good things—none of that qualifies. Romans 12:1 tells us to "Present yourself" and that's what servant leaders are willing to do.

Let's keep it clear and simple. Are you leading yourself faithfully? Are you in love and totally dependent on the wisdom of the Scriptures? Build your leadership life on the Word of God. It gives us the ability to live skillfully.

We are living in uncertain times with uncertain outcomes. You need to anticipate areas of stress and be aware that there will be dark days. Diane and I have been married for almost five decades. I met her in the Jesus Movement when we were 17, and we married very quickly after. God gave me this beautiful Italian girl, who has loved the Lord and been a faithful servant. This year, she faced breast cancer surgery and treatment along with a few complications that put her in ICU for more than a week. That was tough. I'm supposed to be the protector. I could pick up the phone and get her into MD Anderson quickly and arrange the best care, but this last part was out of my hands. Way above my pay grade and it was tough.

I'm not saying, if you live for Jesus, there's never going to be a problem. No, you are going to be squeezed a lot in your life. There may be moments ten times worse. Anticipate periods of stress by understanding how to live faithfully in this modern world. By making the decision to believe the book no matter what. When Diane received that first diagnosis, she posted on her She Loves Out Loud Facebook page, "I will praise you even if the sun refuses to shine." And she has.

All around me I am seeing high-profile spiritual leaders lose their legacy for a dumb decision they made after decades of faithful serving. As one of my favorite authors, Stephen Covey, famously wrote, "Begin with the end in mind."[9]

9 Franklin Covey, *The 7 Habits of Highly Effective People.* Retrieved from https://www.franklincovey.com/habit-2/.

Decide now:

- To sacrifice yourself to reach this generation.
- To live your life according to a biblical worldview no matter what the rest of the world does.
- To become an effective, spiritual, servant leader.
- To be a focused, faithful leader who finishes what he or she is called to begin.

In closing, one of the greatest and most valuable advice I can share is that passion and efforts to reach and keep this generation will bless you beyond measure. "Leverage the wave" is a phrase I learned while surfing on the beaches of Florida as a teen. Doors opened for future ministry with professional sports teams, White House conferences, international ministry and relationships, churches, corporations, and other opportunities I never even imagined. And I am no one special; just a guy who said, "Lord, send me wherever you want me to go."

Right now, you may be wrestling with how to get everything done and still prepare for the future. Many youth ministry leaders delay completing or continuing education because of the daily demands of family and current responsibilities. Fighting these issues myself, I named my podcast "There's always a way." I say to you, "Don't quit trying."

I am so proud to share with you the opportunity for the most exciting youth ministry online education through the Strack Center at Charleston Southern University. From your home or office, you can earn a major or minor right now in youth ministry, leadership, or biblical worldview. Here is our goal—that every course and every week while you are completing the assignment you are finding "smooth stones" for your sling as you prepare for ministry events and counseling. We created this center so you could soar in your ministry with confidence and anointing. The students and the Lord deserve better than good; they deserve excellence.

CHAPTER 11

PREACHING AND TEACHING THE ANCIENT TEXT TO A MODERN STUDENT

Benjamin B. Phillips, Ph.D.

In a world where what is newer is (almost) always better, more desirable, and more valuable, how do you communicate the Ancient Text to modern students? Is the task of the modern preacher or teacher to make the Bible come alive to modern students? If, as the authors of this book have argued, this particular Ancient Text (the Bible) is the Word of God, "living and active, sharper than any two-edged sword" (Hebrews 4:12, ESV), then draw it and charge! There is a time and a place to defend our confidence and trust in this Ancient Text, as we have also done in this book. But when the time comes to communicate the Ancient Text to modern students, demonstrate the confidence of the young Timothy obeying the charge of his mentor, the Apostle Paul, who told him to "Preach the word; be ready in season and out of season; correct, rebuke, and encourage with great patience and teaching" (2 Timothy 4:2, CSB).

Say What the Text Says

One of the core convictions anyone tasked with the teaching or preaching of the Bible should hold is that students need to hear what God has to say far more than they need to hear what we have to say. The Apostle Paul demonstrated this commitment when he insisted that he had,

> renounced secret and shameful things, not acting deceitfully or distorting the word of God, but commending ourselves before God to everyone's conscience by an open display of the truth.... For we are not proclaiming ourselves but Jesus Christ as Lord, and ourselves as your servants for Jesus's sake (2 Corinthians 4:2, 5, CSB).

False teachers not only deny that Jesus is Lord when they explicitly reject His deity or the efficacy of His death and resurrection for salvation. They also elevate themselves to a throne of supreme rule over others when they proclaim their own ideas rather than what God says through His Spirit in Scripture (1 Corinthians 1:18-25).

Preaching and teaching that does not say what the Ancient Text says, no matter how sincere the evangelistic or apologetic motive, is broken by two tragic flaws. First, it exposes the teacher to God's wrath against false prophets (those who say, "Thus says the LORD," when the LORD did not say it; Deuteronomy 18:20). Second, reliance on merely human words (ideas) over the Word of God abandons the faith-creating, life-transforming power of God's Word for the feeble effect of merely human insights and persuasion. Make no mistake, God uses His Word—the Ancient Text—to produce saving, sanctifying faith in modern students (Romans 10:17). God has chosen the foolishness of the preaching and teaching of the Bible as the way He displays His power to save and sanctify (1 Corinthians 1:18).

Saying what the Text says, however, does not limit the speaker to simply quoting Scripture. After the exile in Babylon, Ezra and the Levites read the Word to the people, "giving the meaning so the people could understand what was read" (Nehemiah 8:8, CSB). The authors of the New Testament, speaking through what they wrote, didn't merely quote the Old Testament, but also conveyed its meaning through paraphrasing, explaining, and illustrating it's meaning to those who heard their message. Their writings, inspired and sealed by the Holy Spirit to convey truth without any mixture of error, tell us what God wants us to say.

Most importantly, this means that our task as teachers and preachers of the Ancient Text to modern students is to *say what the Text says* rather than what we might wish it said. It is usually fine to go straight to a text that already, truly says what you feel led to say. On the other hand, it is dangerous to decide what you want to say and then go look for a text that says it. If you try hard enough, you will find a text to support your idea—sometimes even when the text you use doesn't actually say what you are saying!

To combat the danger of elevating human insights and agendas above God's, some teachers choose to work their way through a large block of Scripture (e.g., a chapter, the major section of a book, a whole book) over a period of time. In this strategy, your goal is to teach through a natural unit of text (like a paragraph, a story, etc.) and to help students see the ways in which that particular text intersects the lives of your students. This approach is warranted by the fact that "*ALL* Scripture" (emphasis added) is not only inspired, but ALL of it is also "profitable for teaching, for rebuking, for correcting, [and] for training in righteousness" (2 Timothy 3:16). Granted, it is easier for us to see this in some places in Scripture than in others, but it is always true even if we can't see how it is true for a particular text in Scripture.

Another strategy for *saying what the Text says* is to identify biblical topics, seek texts that speak to those topics, and then say only what that specific text says about your topic. Moving from text to text, each of which adds to our understanding of what the whole Bible has to say on the topic, helps us to continue to "say what the text says" while addressing specific issues of concern in the lives of modern students. This approach is warranted by the example of the New Testament authors, who often brought together multiple passages of the Old Testament to address specific issues among Christians (e.g., sin in Romans 1–3; marriage and family in 1 Corinthians 7). Here it will be safest to look for topics that the Bible itself addresses. The categories of the Ancient Text, like *sin*, *faithfulness*, or *joy* can have some overlap with the categories of modern culture like *mistake*, *success*, or *happiness*. But these biblical concepts also reject some aspects of these modern categories, and always say more than the modern categories say.

Whatever strategy you adopt (and there are others), the goal of anyone who preaches or teaches the Ancient Text to modern students must be to *say what the Text says*. Openly displaying the truth of God's Word, rather than misappropriating its authority to authorize our own independent ideas and insights, is essential to serving faithfully the students whom King Jesus has entrusted to our care and helping them to follow Jesus as Lord rather than us.

The Way the Text Says It

The Ancient Text, being God's written Word, is the source and authority for our message to modern students. Since it tells us what God wants us to say, our task is to *say what the Text says*. But the Scripture does more than just tell us what to say—it also our first and best model for communicating God's Word in any time and place. In other words, we want to *say what the Text says, the way the Text says it*.

As you think about what the Text says, learn to observe *how* the Text says what it says. Some passages lay down the Law through moral codes, instructions for required practices (like sacrifices), or case law (laws about how to handle specific kinds of situations that arise). Others call to mind the family stories of God's faithfulness through time by rattling off the names of all the kinfolk who came before (genealogies). But the three most common kinds of texts in the Bible are: *narratives*, which tell stories (both historical events and parables); *poetry* such as the Psalms and Proverbs; and the *discourses*, which explain and unpack key truths, applying them to real-world situations. Each of these kinds of texts communicate in different ways that can spark the imagination of both preachers and students.

Narratives comprise the largest portion of the Bible, as much as 43% by some estimates. When we try to communicate these narratives by identifying a thesis and points in the story that prove or support the thesis, they can be very difficult to communicate. Just imagine trying to communicate the story of how you fell in love in the form of a lecture! But, when we are sensitive to *the way the Text says it*, narratives become some of the easiest texts to communicate—and the most fun! Most people are used to telling stories; vacation stories, work stories, school and sports stories, even stories about situations that made us (or someone else) look silly! While we can all get better at storytelling, it doesn't take too much practice to become a competent storyteller. Simply tell the story that the Bible tells! Draw the attention of students to key dialogue in the text. Weave in the background information that explains key details the same way you would if you were explaining a part of your vacation to someone who hadn't ever been to the place you visited. Most of all, save the moral of the story for the end. While you may hint at it in the beginning, or raise a question or issue that the moral of the story will address, let the big idea and the application come at the end.

As you consider the big idea that the story is communicating, look for how the story fits into the larger context of the book and into the overall flow of the history that the Bible tells. Do not be content simply to say, "Be like David!" or "Don't be like Saul!" Point out how the story helps us to better understand who God is and how He operates. Ask yourself how the story points to Jesus, whether as the ultimate answer to the problem in the story or as the perfect paradigm of what one or more characters in the story was or should have been. Look for other places in the Bible which refer to the story and use it to illustrate or make a point. These cross-references can help you to see implications in the story that you might have missed, and they help students to get to know the whole Bible better. In the end, remember that stories are the best-remembered elements in most communication. Few people remember the point of last Sunday's sermon, but many remember the stories that were told to illustrate that message. With biblical narratives, the story IS the Scripture!

The second most-common form of writing in the Ancient Text are the poetic passages. While most of us think quickly of the Psalms, it's important to remember that there is poetry found scattered throughout the Bible, especially in the Prophets and in Proverbs. The poetry of the Psalms and the Prophets can seem especially challenging. Does *saying it the way the text says it* require a lesson, devotional, or message delivered as a poem? Thankfully, no (though if you can pull it off, then go for it!). Instead, consider how biblical poetry works, and let that shape your strategy for communicating these ancient texts to modern students.

It may surprise you, but the most natural bridge from communicating biblical narratives to communicating biblical poetry are the proverbs! These compact little texts have been described as "long experiences captured in short sayings." This means that they call to mind stories where the proverb applies. A great strategy for communicating these wise sayings would be to think about stories in the Ancient Text and stories in the world of modern students that illustrate the truth of the proverb. Use the proverb itself as a repeated refrain that articulates the moral of the story for each brief tale you tell. Though proverbs comprise most of the book of Proverbs, you will also find these short wisdom sayings scattered throughout the Ancient Text, especially in Jesus' teaching in the Gospels. Communicating the proverbs of the Ancient Text to modern students allows you to leverage your story-telling strengths while helping students get used to the feel of biblical poetry.

Like most English poetry, the Bible's poetry is full of concrete images and compact language. It's supposed to be savored, like a rib eye or a game-winning shot. Take your time as you read it … don't rush! Unlike most English poetry, the Bible's poetry depends on pairing parallel lines of verse rather than on rhyme or meter. This *parallelism* shows up when the second line restates the idea of the first line with a different image (synonymous parallelism), or when the second line contrasts the first (antithetical parallelism). Sometimes, the second line even completes or develops the idea of the first (synthetic parallelism). These strategies all serve to intensify the ideas being communicated.

When communicating biblical poetry then, don't just point out these images and parallels, think about how to replicate them for your students. Let your tone of voice and the pace with which you speak be tools to convey the impact of the images. Picture a student gushing about a recent trip, then pausing and capping it all off with, "I had fun. It was a blast!" (synonymous parallelism). Or imagine a parent pointing to an empty pizza box and saying, "My son is fifteen," before concluding in love and exasperation, "he inhales food!" (synthetic parallelism). This way of communicating uses vivid images to *show* the idea rather than simply *explaining* what the idea is. Put images together to build the intensity and richness of the picture being painted and the emotions being expressed. As you do, remember that much of the Bible's poetry (especially the Psalms) was meant to be sung—they came with music! So, as you savor the picture being painted, ask yourself, "what is the soundtrack to this text?" Think about the songs or kinds of music familiar to your students that capture the message or the emotion of the text (and best, capture both!). Music can set up the message or even be part of it.

The third-largest category of texts in the Bible are the ones we turn to most often and most quickly for preaching and teaching; the discourses, or teaching texts. Here we think of the letters of the New Testament, and some parts of the Old Testament prophets. Teaching texts can be short (a paragraph or two) or quite long (a whole chapter or more). They commonly take the form of a monologue (a discourse) on a particular subject or idea. Some discourses were delivered directly through speech to a group of people who gathered to hear the speaker (these were written down later), others started out in written form (like the New Testament epistles) and were intended to be read aloud to a gathered group. Either way, the discourses allow us to overhear Jesus, Isaiah, John, Jeremiah, Peter, or Paul making a point with depth and (typically) without being interrupted.

The discourses of the Ancient Text are not, however, mere lectures. Sensitivity to how the discourses say what they say will help you to notice when they weave in other kinds of texts like proverbs (e.g., 1 Peter 5:7) and poems/hymns (e.g., Philippians 2:5-11). Here you can take advantage of how those kinds of texts communicate as a component part of your preaching/teaching of the discourse.

Discourses also call to mind specific narratives in Scripture when they use them to illustrate a point. Naming a key figure from the Old Testament narratives should lead us to think of the stories in which the person appeared and how they demonstrated (or failed to demonstrate!) the truth being discussed in the discourse. Discourses also will make much more frequent use of quotes and allusions to earlier parts of Scripture than narratives do. Modern students *get* allusions and quotes from movies and songs, sometimes referencing a whole scene, story, or character across multiple movies with a single line! They are able to do this because they know these stories and songs so well; much more than they do the stories and songs of the Ancient Text. Here is another way in which preaching and teaching the narratives and poetry of Scripture can really pay off. When necessary, you can pause and recap the ancient story or song. But the greatest impact of these quick references happens when students get it without explanation—like a joke that works best when you don't have to explain it after you've told it! As a result, you might lay a foundation for preaching or teaching a discourse beforehand by helping students to know, enjoy, and remember the stories and songs referenced by the discourse you will be preaching/teaching sometime in the near future.

Conclusion

The Ancient Text is composed of many different types of texts, from narrative, to poetry, to discourse, and many more. Each of these have their own ways of communicating God's Word to everyone the Ancient Text encounters, including modern students. As you dive into *what* the Text says you will become more and more faithful in helping your students hear what God has to say to them (rather than merely your own opinions). As you see more and more clearly *how* the Text says what it says, you will become more and more creative and fresh in your own communication of that message.

Our task is not to make the Bible come alive to modern students. Like a tiger in the jungle or a shark in the sea, the Ancient Text is a powerful and skilled hunter, supreme in its domain. Different texts may hunt in different ways, but every text in this greatest of Ancient Texts is *"inspired by God and is profitable for teaching, for rebuking, for correcting, for training in righteousness, so that the* [modern student] *may be complete, equipped for every good work"* (2 Timothy 3:16–17, CSB). The miracle is not just that the Ancient Text transforms modern students. It is an equally wondrous miracle that modern preachers and teachers get to be part of what God is using His Ancient Text to do in modern students.

CHAPTER 12

DISCIPLING THE HEART OF A MODERN STUDENT

Jonathan D. Denton, Ph.D.

The joy of gardening is the harvesting. As I mentioned earlier, we live near a working farm. The farm has u-pick seasons and we love to go as a family and pick things like strawberries, blueberries, grapes, and peaches. Our two boys love these days and probably eat as much as they pick! Some of our favorite pictures of our boys are of them in the fields with strawberry juice just dripping off their faces. As we pick, we teach them what a ripe fruit looks like so that they pick the right ones. They also know to avoid the bad fruit.

As we minister to students, the joy is in seeing the good fruit in their life. As I write this, I am at a summer camp with junior high students. As to be expected with this age group, we are seeing some bad fruit like discipline issues, disrespect to leaders, and unwise behavior. But we are also seeing lots of good fruit like salvation, discipleship, wise decisions, community building, and serving others.

Jesus states in Luke 6:43-45,

> A good tree doesn't produce bad fruit; on the other hand, a bad tree doesn't produce good fruit. For each tree is known by its

own fruit. Figs aren't gathered from thornbushes, or grapes picked from a bramble bush. A good person produces good out of the good stored up in his heart. An evil person produces evil out of the evil stored up in his heart, for his mouth speaks from the overflow of the heart (CSB).

The Ancient Text is not just a good story for our students to know. The Ancient Text is the seed that transforms the heart of a student. The work of the Ancient Text in the life of a student results in spiritual fruit.

Our Current Bad Fruit

Whenever there is bad fruit, something wrong has happened. The soil wasn't right, the plant didn't get enough or too much water or sun, or there weren't enough nutrients for the plant. When we look at the lives of students today, we are beginning to see the fruit of the modern world in their lives. As Jesus stated, "For each tree is known by its own fruit."

Dr. Jackson stated earlier that students today live after the "game-changers" of the changing family, moral relativism, hopelessness, and media influence.[1] With the soil of the changing family, we now minister to students who come from a variety of family backgrounds. Some students are living with the fruit of hurt from divorce, abuse, or fatherlessness. These students may be easily angered or easily hurt. Some students live with the fruit of multiple home environments as they spend every other week in different homes. One parent may be discipling them toward Christlikeness and one parent may be discipling toward worldly behavior. Students may also be displaying the fruit of confusion in their life because of the changing family. I know of a student whose dad left the family, began a relationship with another man, and moved into a house with his partner down the street from the student. How does a student who is beginning abstract thinking process this?

---

[1] See Chapter 6, page 77.

With the soil of moral relativism, students are beginning to display the fruit of individualist thinking. The game-changer is that Christian students used to have the worldview that they exist in a God-created, God-defined world. In this world, the main goal of the student was to love and honor the God who created the world and align their life to Him. Now, students grow up in a world that is a me-created, me-defined world. Carl Trueman states the shift is that now people see the world as "raw material out of which meaning and purpose can be created by the individual."[2] A me-directed, me-defined world places the individual at the center and thus leads to the individual as "sovereign."[3] The fruit of the "individual as sovereign" leads students to build their brand through social media, cheer on their friends who define their gender, move freely from religious group to religious group, and pursue majors and careers because they like what it offers and not because God calls them to it.

The individual as sovereign goes directly against the Word of God which presents God as sovereign. As the psalter states in Psalm 103:15-19:

> As for man, his days are like grass—he blooms like a flower of the field; when the wind passes over it, it vanishes, and its place is no longer known. But from eternity to eternity the LORD's faithful love is toward those who fear him, and his righteousness toward the grandchildren of those who keep his covenant, who remember to observe his precepts. The LORD has established his throne in heaven, and his kingdom rules over all (CSB).

The Ancient Text reminds us that the modern student vanishes quickly but the Lord is sovereign.

With the soil of hopelessness, we are now seeing a generation of students who are displaying the fruit of anxiety. In 2020, Barna found that 26% of Gen Z teens and young adults feel anxious. The

---

[2] Carl Trueman, *The Rise and Triumph of the Modern* Self (Wheaton: Crossway, 2020), 39.
[3] Trueman, 50.

article states, "About one in four members of Gen Z meets the criteria for empowered (25%) or anxious (26%). Their inherent desire for success and the accompanying weight of expectations seem to push them toward one of two extremes—anxiety or empowerment—or, for a small percentage (5%), some fusion of these seemingly incongruent emotions."[4] Following the COVID-19 pandemic, the CDC found that over a third (37%) of high school students reported poor mental health during the pandemic and almost half (44%) felt persistently sad or hopeless.[5]

Even before the pandemic, anxiety was on the rise among teenagers. I attended a church's fall retreat weekend with high school students in 2019. During the classic Saturday night share time around the camp bonfire, about 40 of the 100 students shared. Every single testimony of the 40 included some form of this statement: "A couple of years ago I was struggling with anxiety/depression." Some even included severe depression and suicidal thoughts. These are affluent students with incredible opportunities and material wealth, yet they were all struggling with anxiety/depression.

We are also seeing the rise of anxiety in our college classrooms. I teach youth ministry classes at a Christian college. I also teach Old and New Testament survey classes which are a required core class for all our students. I began noticing that every semester I was having more and more accommodation plans for students in my classes with anxiety. I reached out to our school counselor to ask why he thought we were having so many accommodations for

---

[4] "New Data on Gen Z—Perceptions of Pressure, Anxiety and Empowerment," Barna, 28 January 2021, Retrieved 17 July, 2022 from https://www.barna.com/research/gen-z-success.

[5] "New CDC data illuminate youth mental health threats during the COVID-19 pandemic," CDC, 31 March 2022, https://www.cdc.gov/media/releases/2022/p0331-youth-mental-health-covid-19.html (accessed 17 July 2022). NOTE: In February 2023, the CDC released a report that COVID was not as significant a factor in teen mental health as supposed, "Youth Risk Behavior Survey," CDC, 13 February 2023, https://www.cdc.gov/healthyyouth/data/yrbs/pdf/YRBS_Data-Summary-Trends_Report2023_508.pdf (accessed 23 February 2023). Also see: "The new CDC report shows that Covid added little to teen mental health trends" https://jonathanhaidt.substack.com/p/the-new-cdc-report (accessed 23 February 2023).

anxiety. He brought up the fact that we are having a widening gap. In one sense, the modern world is causing anxious thoughts through heavier fears and worry. Also, more and more students are being diagnosed with anxiety disorders. At the same time, the skills needed to handle worries and fear are decreasing. Thus, the gap between normal fears and worries/anxiety disorders and the skills to handle them is becoming larger and larger. I am impressed with our students who are getting help because they tell me all the new skills they are learning to handle their anxiety. Yet, I am still regularly getting emails from students telling me that they tried to come to class, had an anxiety attack on the way, and had to go back to their room. When we see the soil of the modern world, the lack of the seed of the Ancient Text, the lack of gardeners, then we see the fruit of anxiety wreaking havoc in the lives of our students.

Finally, with the soil of media influence we are now seeing the fruit that technology and media produces. First, students live in a world of multiple screens. My firstborn son is about to be a sixth grader. He was working on his summer reading project today on his computer while his tablet was next to him playing YouTube kids and the television was on. If something is not gripping their attention, students today simply switch screens or change apps. One of the dangers is that religion will just become another thing in their life that they look to for a moment and then switch to something else. Second, students are faced with a major temptation, especially with social media, to brand themselves. They create themselves on social media and then they have to live up to that creation. This pressure is amplified with comments and likes. They also see the creation of others and judge themselves against that creation.

Producing Good Fruit

So how do we produce good fruit in the lives of students? Paul instructs Timothy to pastor as a soldier, athlete, and farmer. These three images give a picture of what it looks like to disciple the heart of a modern student

Build Discipleship/Care Ministries Centered on God's Word. As a soldier, Paul reminds Timothy that "No one serving as a soldier gets entangled in the concerns of civilian life; he seeks to please the commanding officer" (2 Timothy 2:4, CSB). As we minister to students it is so easy to get wrapped up in all the cultural issues and trends and build ministries to address the cultural moment. While it is important to study the needs of the culture, we must remember that the only lasting change we will see in students is only if our ministries are built on God's Word. God is not thrown off by the cultural moment. As we read Scripture, we see that God works both in Israel and Babylon. He works in Jerusalem and Athens. As Mordecai tells Esther, "If you keep silent at this time, relief and deliverance will come to the Jewish people from another place, but you and your father's family will be destroyed. Who knows, perhaps you have come to your royal position for such a time as this" (Esther 4:14, CSB). Just like Esther came to her place at the exact right time, so also our students today exist because God has placed them in this moment. If God is their creator, then we want to make sure we are listening to Him about how to build our student ministries. Often, I find myself building my ministry off the latest idea or book. While we should always be learning, growing, and fine-tuning our ministries, the core of what we do must be built off the Ancient Text.

In order to build our ministries off the commander's Word through the Ancient Text we must, first, place the gospel at the center of all that we do., While I love new ideas about ministry, I have learned to begin thinking about ministry through God's Word first. In my introduction class for student ministry at CSU, I begin with two books that provide a biblical basis for doing student ministry.[6] I want my student ministry students to start thinking about ministry through a God-centered philosophy and not just a pragmatic philosophy. Everything we do in ministry and teaching should be

---

[6] *Gospel-Centered Youth Ministry: A Practical Guide* edited by Cameron Cole and Jon Nielson and *Student Ministry by the Book: Biblical Foundations for Student Ministry* by Ed Newton and R. Scott Pace.

rooted in the gospel, God's mission for the church, and discipleship. We build our programs to fulfill the mission of the church and as instructed through passages such as Deuteronomy 6, Matthew 28, and Acts 2.

Second, we must view our students as God defines a student. All students are created in the image of God with honor and value. We must start our understanding of students here, even the tough-to-love kids! While students are created in the image of God, we also know that all our students are fallen because of their sinful nature and choices. They are not just in need of a fresh coat of paint. The core of their spiritual house is broken and in need of repair. Students are not inherently good or blank slates for us to write on. They have a sinful condition that leads to sinful behaviors. Thus, students need redemption through the work of Christ. The onramp of discipleship is presenting the gospel message to students and helping them clearly understand the nature of salvation. When a student joined our church as a new believer, I met weekly with the student for three weeks going back over the basics of salvation, what took place, and how the student can grow in their new relationship with Christ. I saw this as the onramp for discipleship and then connected them to small groups. And finally, students who have a relationship with Christ are heading toward a final restoration. We get to disciple and minister to them between these two important moments: salvation and restoration.

Be a Leader Worth Imitating. Paul also instructs Timothy to disciple others like an athlete. He reminds Timothy "if anyone competes as an athlete, he is not crowned unless he competes according to the rules" (2 Timothy 2:5, CSB). Student ministers and those who work with students today must be above reproach. The world is closely scrutinizing us because of the moral failures of a few. But this cannot be why we strive to be people of strong moral character. We strive to minister with strong Christian character because of the call that God has placed in our lives. Our students are impressionable and often they learn just as much from observing our lives as from our teaching. I had a parent once come up to me and thank me for the way that I handled a conflict. She thanked me because her son had watched the way that I handled the conflict (I did not even know he was watching!) and he had told her what he learned about conflict resolution from watching. This also means that as we build our student ministry volunteer team we must build it on people of character and not just on popularity. One of my favorite passages of Scripture to illustrate student ministry is 1 Thessalonians 1:4-7. Paul writes,

> For we know, brothers loved by God, that he has chosen you, because our gospel came to you not only in word, but also in power and in the Holy Spirit and with full conviction. You know what kind of men we proved to be among you for your sake. And you became imitators of us and of the Lord, for you received the word in much affliction, with the joy of the Holy Spirit, so that you became an example to all the believer sin Macedonia and in Achaia (ESV).

Paul shared the gospel with the Word of God to the Thessalonians. Paul also shared the gospel through the power of God's work in their lives and churches. And Paul shared the gospel through how he lived the gospel. He lived out the gospel in his life in front of the Thessalonians. They then imitated his life and were examples to others. When I read this passage early in my ministry career, I learned the importance of not only sharing the gospel from a stage, but also through my life. Be a youth minister/leader/teacher worth a student following your example.

Disciple/Care for Students Through a Strategic Plan. Finally, Paul instructs Timothy to disciple others and care for others as a farmer. Paul states, "the hardworking farmer ought to be the first to get a share of the crops." (2 Timothy 2:6. CSB). My grandfather was a dairy farmer and I remember loving to go to the farm and help him. There was always something to do. Every day the animals had to be taken care of and plants needed to be tended to. Sometimes we put up hay and sometimes it was simply riding around the property and checking on everything. Even at Christmas, we could not open our presents until my grandfather finished all of the daily tasks of the farm. As we disciple students, the work we do is continuous and hard. We often think that the change we want to see in our students will happen in one lesson or one event. God sometimes will do great things in these moments, but discipleship often comes through multiple lessons over a long period of time.

Farmers work hard tending to their plants so that the plant will produce good fruit. We can use the word FARMER as a way to look at how to care for the hearts of our students. As a FARMER, we:

F – Find the soil and root conditions

A – Ask how the gospel applies

R – Research modern issues and problems

M – Make relational pipelines

E – Enter the gospel

R – Repent or Respond

First, we disciple and care for our students by seeking to find the soil and root condition of their hearts. I began my ministry to students by thinking my sole job was to pump as much biblical knowledge as I could into my students. I expected that all that Bible knowledge would translate into good behavior. I expected to reach the head and then the hands would follow. We all know how that turns out. My problem was that I bypassed the heart. Over time, I learned that reaching the heart of a student is an important part of ministry. As Proverbs 4:23 states, "Guard your heart above all else, for it is the source of life" (CSB).

Finding the soil and root condition of a student's heart takes time. One way that we can do this is to look for windows into our students' hearts. One of the best ways that I found to do this was to make sure that all my administrative tasks were done before any student walked onto our campus or into my group. That way, I was free to greet students and ask them about their days. Often, these conversations give us so many windows into their hearts. Sometimes they are excited about their day and their excitement tells us about their passions. And sometimes they are frustrated and these frustrations will often tell us about idols in their hearts. Another way that we can find the soil and root condition of a student's heart is to learn to ask good questions. Students will talk if we ask open-ended questions that are not leading questions. For example, my fellow 8th-grade guys small group leaders and I have learned not to ask: "How was your day?" That question will always end in "good." Instead, we ask "What was your high? What was your low? And what was your uh-oh?" These are much better questions because students must look back over their day and evaluate the moments of the day. We get much better information from questions like these.

Second, we ask how the gospel applies. This is the part where we want to make sure we understand the main story of the Ancient Text, which is why so much time was spent on the Ancient Text at the beginning of this book. If not, we will approach Bible in the wrong way. Paul David Tripp wisely states:

> Many Christians simply don't understand what the Bible is. Many think of it as a spiritual encyclopedia: God's complete catalog of human problems, coupled with a complete list of divine answers. If you turn to the right page, you can find answers for any struggle.... This kind of ministry rarely leads to lasting change because it does not bring the power of the Word to the places where change is really needed. In this kind of ministry, self is still at the center, personal need is the focus, and personal happiness remains the goal. But a truly effective ministry of the Word must confront our self-focus and self-absorption at its roots, opening us up to the vastness of a God-defined, God-centered world. Unless this happens, we will use the promises,

principles, and commands of the Word to serve the thing we really love: ourselves.[7]

I was so convicted when I read this statement from Tripp. It is so tempting to approach the Bible looking for the answers we want for ourselves and our students. But instead of helping them, we are actually pushing them further into a *me-defined, me-centered* world. Our students need a bigger story for their life—a story that is "God-defined, God-centered."

Third, we research modern issues and problems. We should periodically take time to study modern issues and problems that our students may face. This can be reading news articles, journal articles, books, and cultural websites. We also need a few pastoral counseling books that can help us when students have specific issues they are facing. We have to learn to be ok asking a student if we can get back together in a few days so that we can research issues that we are not familiar with. This is much better than just guessing an action plan.

Fourth, we make relational pipelines. As we ask questions and discuss issues with our students, we do so by building relational connections. One way that we can do this is to appropriately share from our own life. As someone wisely said, "vulnerability leads to vulnerability." We also want to encourage our students in things that they are doing well. And we want to listen with empathy as our students share. All of this creates a pipeline from our hearts to the heart of a student.

Fifth, once the pipeline from our heart to the heart of a student is established, then we enter the gospel. A lot of times, we want to listen quickly and then give all of our biblical knowledge. I especially struggle with wanting to give all the answers quickly because I am a teacher, minister, and guy. But I have had to learn to listen well, ask good questions, and pray about what to share. Once the pipeline

---

[7] Paul David Tripp, *Instruments in the Redeemer's Hands* (Phillipsburg, New Jersey: P&R Publishing Company, 2002), 24-25.

is created and we are sure what the root issue is, then we want to pour all the gospel we can into the heart of our students. Listening and showing empathy does not mean that we minimize the gospel. Instead, we rightly apply the gospel in ways that our students will actually listen because we are applying it to their heads and their hearts.

And finally, we help our students repent or respond. As we rightly apply the gospel to our students' lives, it will always lead to change in their lives. Sometimes it will lead them to repentance. Other times it will lead them to respond differently in the future. Sometimes it will lead them to repair a relationship. The gospel will always lead to change and our last task is to help our students think through what changes need to be made.

If we walk our students through these steps, we will often see real fruit produced in their lives. One of my greatest joys is serving in student ministry long enough that I am now seeing fruit years down the road. Students that I discipled and counseled are now married and parenting their children well. When we plant well from the ground up, the fruit will continue to produce years down the road like a fruit tree.

CHAPTER 13

INTEGRATING OUR ANCIENT TEXT INTO EDUCATION AND MINISTRY

Michael Bryant, Ph.D.

Introduction

I have taught students in Christian schools and churches for more than twenty-five years. Some of the wisest words of counsel given to me by my seminary professors and pastor mentors was the importance of modeling a ministry closely tied to Scripture. By this my professors and pastors meant that whether in an academic or local church context, my efforts should reflect a sincere commitment to integrate the Scriptures.

This chapter will seek to assist Bible teachers and student pastors in integrating God's Word into the lives of students by addressing the question, "What are some helpful principles to consider when attempting to integrate the Bible into an education program for a modern student, whether in a Christian school or the local church?" For our purposes, integration refers to offering an education program in which the Bible permeates *every* aspect of student learning.[1] Furthermore, the term education refers to elements related to the learning or discipleship experience in a Christian school or the local church.

Bible teachers in a Christian school and student ministers in the local church serve in different contexts. Nevertheless, both employ the same tool and pursue broadly a similar goal. Their tool is the Bible, and their goal is to produce authentic Christian disciples.

Principles for Integration

Prioritize the Bible. Integrating the Bible into one's education program requires prioritizing it above all other concerns. Most Christian educators and student pastors would agree that placing the Bible first is essential for effective integration. Nevertheless, when they actually attempt to do this, real-world challenges such as people and their perspectives, institutional culture, and popular trends may result in Scripture being deprioritized.

Administrators, faculty, and parents in Christian schools as well as pastoral leaders and members in churches are usually well-meaning. Nevertheless, at times their perspectives or approaches may fail to incorporate essential biblical principles (or even contradict them). A school or church's institutional culture may have followed unbiblical practices for years, thus making implementing biblical principles challenging. Popular trends, which some may regard as irrefutable best practices, can also present challenges. A Christian educator or student pastor may feel great pressure to use a best practice other schools or churches are currently using due to its positive results.[2]

---

[1] Biblical integration is more than merely including the Bible in a chapel service or Wednesday evening student ministry meeting.

[2] Some best practices are driven by pragmatic concerns, namely, a focus on results. A negative example of allowing pragmatism to guide one's program would include using non-Christian or even anti-Christian approaches simply because they result in increases in student enrollment or participation.

One practical recommendation for evaluating whether one's program prioritizes the Bible is to ask a number of critical questions. Does the education program (any part) conflict with Scripture? Is it consistent with Scripture's goals for education? What has been the result in students' lives when the school or church implemented a given approach? Did implementation produce biblical disciples? What theological perspective(s) undergird(s) the program? In what ways are certain individuals or groups within the institution influencing the education program? How would you or others within the school or church define the institutional culture? Does the culture reflect biblical values? Which ones? How would you or others within the institution describe its stated approach for educating students? What trends are currently influencing your education program? Who outside the institution can help you to assess whether your education program prioritizes the Bible in light of the above-mentioned factors? Who could conduct an objective review?

Prioritizing the Bible within one's education program can be done, but it requires trust, discernment, and listening to people inside and outside the institution. A Christian educator or student minister must trust Scripture above all other things. When we trust God's Word, we demonstrate we believe it to be true. In addition, a Christian educator or student minister must ask critical questions that assist with discerning where a program is (or should be). Asking questions shows a commitment to wise stewardship. Finally, listening to different perspectives demonstrates humility and an openness to learn from others.

Reflect on the Bible's purposes for education. A second principle that assists Christian educators and student pastors in integrating the Bible into their education program is to reflect on Scripture's purposes for education.[3] By reflecting on these purposes, Christian educators and student ministers can prepare an education program guided by goals that are consistent with Scripture's

---

[3] Though most texts reviewed do not refer to education in a formal setting (i.e., school), activities such as instructing, learning, and formation are implicitly present, especially given the fact that all of God's Word is given for the instruction of His people.

intentions for students' spiritual, intellectual, and ethical formation.

The Old Testament suggests many purposes for education. The Torah shows that education serves to instruct believers so they will reverence the Lord, keep His commands, and thus experience divine blessing (e.g., Deuteronomy 6:1-3). In addition, the Torah emphasizes the importance of God's people being in a covenant relationship with Him, living a specific way, and bearing witness to Him (e.g., Exodus 19:5-6; 20:1-17). The Prophetic Writings demonstrate how God's divine words often challenge and disrupt human thinking and behavior (e.g., Ezekiel 4–6; Malachi 1–2). Finally, the Wisdom literature suggests that an important purpose of education is to teach the young how to live wisely (e.g., Proverbs 1:8; 2:1; 3:1), that is, how to follow the path of God's divine wisdom as opposed to the path of the foolish (e.g., Psalm 1).

The New Testament suggests multiple purposes of education, including: students coming to love God and others wholeheartedly (Matthew 22:37-39); obeying the Great Commission by making disciples who follow Jesus' teachings (Matthew 28:19-20); equipping God's people for service and maturity (Ephesians 4:11-16; Colossians 1:28); renewing believers' minds (Ephesians 4:23); encouraging them to mature in Christ (who is their standard) and to recognize His authority (Ephesians 4:15-16; Colossians 1:28-29; 2:6-7); motivating them to abandon their old life of sin and imitate God's example of true righteousness and holiness (Ephesians 4:24; see also verses 17-23); developing specific virtues within the student as well as avoiding distinctive vices (e.g., Galatians 5:19-23)[4]; striving to pass on sound doctrine (1 Timothy 1:10; 6:3; 2 Timothy 1:13; Titus 1:9), which includes the truth of the gospel (e.g., 1 Timothy 1:11); and combating theological and moral error (e.g., 1 Timothy 1:3-4, 9-10; 2 Timothy 3:1-9).

---

[4] The New Testament writings include lists that have come to be known as "virtue lists" (e.g., Galatians 5:22-23; James 3:17-18; 2 Peter 1:5-7) and "vice lists" (e.g., Galatians 5:19-21; Romans 1:29-31; 1 Corinthians 6:9-10) that identify acceptable and unacceptable behaviors and attitudes for believers.

By reflecting on the Bible's purposes for education, an educator or student minister receives clear guidance regarding the goals that should direct their education program. For instance, as suggested above, the Wisdom Literature emphasizes the importance of imparting practical insights for wise living (e.g., refraining from anger, controlling one's tongue), and the virtue lists teach that learning involves more than transferring knowledge; it should also shape students' character and attitudes (e.g., the fruit of the Spirit). Many of these goals could be integrated into the larger education program or a class's curriculum as objectives to be pursued.

Develop a personal philosophy of education. Another principle for integrating the Bible into one's educational program is to develop a personal philosophy of education informed by Scripture.[5] It is standard practice for a teacher or student minister to prepare a philosophy of education. If you already have a philosophy of education, let me encourage you to strengthen it. If you do not have a philosophy of education, begin working on one. Preparing a philosophy of education will result in an educator or student minister offering a more biblical, balanced, and mature education program. Even an educator or student pastor who has served for years would benefit from revising their philosophy of education. In returning to it, they will likely discover the need for more mature theological thinking on a given topic or realize that some matters previously neglected now require attention due to new challenges in society and culture.

To develop a personal philosophy of education that integrates Scripture, an educator or student minister may begin small by preparing a concise philosophy consisting of foundational topics. For example:

Christ – Christian education should be Christ-centered, directing students' learning so that they recognize His identity as the

---

[5] As already mentioned, the Bible must stand as the ultimate source of authority for one's education program. Nevertheless, along with the Bible, a well-constructed philosophy of education should also incorporate insights from God's truth as found in His general revelation, the Christian intellectual tradition, and current thinking on education and ministry.

Messiah (Matthew 1:1; 16:16), the Son of God (Mark 1:1; 15:39), the Savior (Luke 2:11, 2:30-32; 3:6; 19:10), the divine Word and Creator (John 1:1-3), and the cosmic Christ who reigns supreme over His creation (Colossians 1:15-20).

Student – All students are created in God's divine image (Genesis 1:26-27). This truth implies that teachers should treat their students with dignity and respect and view them as possessing the capacity to learn according to God's gifting. Teaching guided by the belief that students bear God's divine image has the power to transform even the poorest students into learners.

Educator/Student Pastor – In addition to demonstrating teaching excellence, Christian educators and student pastors should display godly character (e.g., 1 Timothy 3:1-7), seek to glorify God (1 Corinthians 10:31), promote biblical discipleship (Matthew 28:19-20), provide guidance to students for evaluating their world, and encourage a wholehearted love for God and others (Matthew 22:37-39), as their personal example will influence students (Luke 6:40).

Learning Environment – Christian educators and student pastors must establish a context that is conducive to the learning objectives of the institution in general and authentic Christian discipleship in particular. Moreover, students need to feel valued and safe as they are encouraged to develop spiritually, cognitively, emotionally, and socially.

The examples discussed above are merely representative of the topics that one might include initially in a philosophy of education.[6] Later, as one gains new insights through additional teaching, learning, and study, their personal philosophy of education may be expanded.

A personal philosophy of education that integrates Scripture is an invaluable resource. This simple tool has the potential to strengthen one's efforts by incorporating the richness and diversity of

---

[6] A more developed philosophy of education should be prepared and include topics such as truth, sin, curriculum, outcomes, and assessment.

Scripture's teachings into an education program.[7] In fact, without a well-written philosophy of education that draws from the entire canon, a Christian educator or student ministry may be tempted to allow one or two biblical themes to dominate their efforts. As a result, the educator or student minister may unintentionally create a personal canon within the larger biblical canon, thus neglecting the total truth of Scripture.[8]

Align integration efforts in smaller units with the institution's stated Christian identity and distinctive education model. Effective biblical integration requires an educator or student minister to reflect carefully on how individual departments or smaller units within an institution (i.e., school or church) relate to the school or church's articulated Christian identity and education model. For example, a Christian high school education program for seniors should align with the school's stated mission, vision, values, and education approach (e.g., educating the whole student), while a program for high school seniors in a local church should be consistent with the church's faith statement, core values, Christian tradition, and model. Appropriate alignment of the smaller unit with the institution's stated identity and model will result in a more consistent integration of Scripture.

To achieve alignment, consider asking these questions: What biblical teachings are articulated in the institution's larger Christian identity (e.g., mission, vision, core values)? How well do the smaller units' (i.e., individual programs) reflect these teachings? How might the teachings be more clearly and consistently articulated across the institution? What type of graduate or disciple does

---

[7] Helpful resources for learning more about writing a philosophy of Christian education include Michael J. Anthony and Warren S. Benson's *Exploring the History and Philosophy of Christian Education: Principles for the 21st Century* (Wipf and Stock, 2011) and William R. Yount's *Created to Learn: A Christian Teacher's Introduction to Educational Psychology*, 2nd ed. (Broadman and Holman, 2010).

[8] A popular practice among some Christians is to adopt a life verse, that is, a single passage of Scripture that identifies one's goals, commitments, or desires for his or her Christian life. While there is nothing wrong with this practice, taken to an extreme, it can result in one neglecting the Bible's rich and diverse intentions for a believer.

the school or church attempt to produce? What does the end product look like? Think specifically in terms of knowledge, virtues (e.g., character, attitudes), and skills? Are the individual programs consistent with the larger institution's articulation of the so-called end product? What about the education model or approach employed across the institution? Is there clear consistency?

Rigid uniformity is not possible due to the uniqueness of some units and the age differences of students. Nevertheless, attempting to align as appropriate the integration efforts of smaller units with the institution's stated Christian identity and education model will result in greater consistency.

Encourage teachers and student pastors to be lifelong learners of the Bible. While all serious efforts to integrate the Bible into a school or church's education program should consider standard issues such as strategy, the learning environment, and intended student outcomes, it is also important to recognize that the quality of a student's learning, whether in a school or church, is directly related to those who teach and disciple. In my own life, my personal progress as a student in a school or disciple in the local church has in many ways been determined by my teacher or student pastor's commitment to grow in their understanding of the Bible. Teachers and student pastors who took steps to mature in their knowledge and application of God's Word contributed significantly to my spiritual, intellectual, and moral development. I learned because they took the steps to grow.

If you are serious about integrating the Bible into the lives of your students, seek to be a lifelong learner of Scripture. Growth may be acquired by pursuing a formal degree (e.g., M.Div.) or certification, participating in a professional organization (e.g., Evangelical Theological Society), examining how similar institutions integrate the Bible (e.g., healthy, growing school or church), learning from a mentor to enhance key skills or expertise (e.g., teaching, writing, curriculum design), or engaging in personal learning (e.g., reading recommended books related to Scripture).

Teachers and student pastors committed to growing in their understanding of the Bible are driven by a sense of calling. They recognize that the Lord has called them to serve Him and others in a specific context (school or church) and they understand that their calling includes being a lifelong learner of Scripture.[9]

Teach students the Bible's essentials for their cultural context. Another principle for those who desire to integrate the Bible into their education program is to teach students Scripture's essentials for their unique cultural context. Here I am merely recommending that educators and student pastors help students understand the Bible's wisdom for their life. While educators and student pastors will likely differ as to what constitutes the essential teachings of Scripture, putting this principle into practice will require one to think through what is most important for students to learn in light of current moral and cultural challenges and to incorporate this material into an education program. Biblical essentials might include: the gospel (e.g., 1 Corinthians 15:3-5), the authority of the Bible, the sanctity of life; Scripture's view of marriage and human sexuality; and the Bible's answers to life's timeless questions (e.g., Where did humans come from? Why are we here? What happens when we die?).

The purpose of mentioning this principle is not to identify a comprehensive list of biblical essentials. Rather, the aim is to encourage educators and student pastors to think strategically regarding how to integrate the Bible into the lives of students under their stewardship. Effective biblical integration should be contextual and relevant to students.

---

[9] Substantive learning requires an educator or student pastor to prepare a plan for development. One could identify an area where he needs to grow in his knowledge or skills, then devise the path for growth. For example, if a student pastor who feels that his ability to counsel students who struggle with anxiety and depression is lacking, he could take one or two courses in biblical counseling from a seminary. Or he could pursue a degree in Christian counseling.

Teach students how to disciple themselves and others. Think in terms of present-future discipleship. In the principle mentioned above related to reflecting on the Bible's purposes for education, I referenced the goal of making disciples (Matthew 28:19-20). Our discipleship efforts should entail teaching students to obey Christ's commands and to conform to His example, but they should also look beyond the present to the future so that those we disciple will be equipped to disciple others. In short, we must view our discipleship efforts as a present-future work.[10] How might this be done? At a minimum it entails helping students understand that their discipleship has a greater purpose beyond their own spiritual development. As the Lord allows, they will one day equip new or younger believers to grow in their faith. Ideally, as educators and student pastors provide their students with a broader understanding of discipleship, the students will form a sense of personal responsibility to learn biblical truth and model godly behavior and virtues.

In addition to expanding students' view of their personal discipleship, an educator and student minister should identify the specific knowledge to be taught and the fundamental skills to be mastered.[11] Knowledge might include the essentials of the gospel, the characteristics of a disciple, and the tasks or duties of a disciple. Skills might include how to read and apply the Scriptures faithfully and responsibly.

Finally, educators and student ministers should provide students whom they are currently discipling the opportunity to disciple others now. Students will learn best by attempting to demonstrate or model what they are taught.

---

[10] Paul's admonition to Timothy (2 Timothy 2:2) shows that our discipleship efforts should be future-oriented. We should entrust biblical truth to faithful students who will themselves be equipped to disciple others. Present discipleship prepares students for future discipleship.

[11] Offering selected classes (school) or teaching sessions (church) such as Survey of the Old Testament, Survey of the New Testament, Bible Interpretation, Christian Discipleship, Biblical Worldview, and Basic Christian Doctrines might serve as means for communicating specific knowledge.

Hire teachers and student ministers who are called and equipped. One of the most important principles to follow when seeking to integrate the Bible into the educational program of a Christian school or local church is to hire Christian educators and student ministers who are called and equipped. Strategies, philosophies of education, and financial resources are crucial for offering a quality program; nevertheless, biblical integration will be limited unless a teacher or student minister has a sense of calling and has taken steps to prepare for their role.[12]

What does it mean to hire teachers and student ministers who are called and equipped? At the most basic level, it means to hire individuals who have sensed God's leadership through His Word, the church, and divine gifting toward a role that entails teaching students how to be faithful disciples who produce faithful disciples. Furthermore, these individuals have taken steps to pursue education that they might be better prepared to communicate Scripture's truth to students.

A sense of calling does not necessarily imply that one has heard an audible voice or seen a blinding light, and being equipped does not always require a formal degree for every role, such as a volunteer role in the local church. Nevertheless, being called and equipped are two important benchmarks for hiring the most effective Christian educators and student ministers. Calling will influence factors such as work ethic and passion for the role, while being appropriately equipped will affect the education and discipleship outcomes for students (Luke 6:40).

---

[12] Most churches would not call a non-Christian to serve as a student minister. However, some Christian schools at times are more open to hiring non-Christian educators due to the struggle to find qualified faculty and meet accreditation standards. While recognizing the challenges Christian schools face, an educator's personal relationship with Christ directly influences his or her ability to provide an authentic Christian education. I strongly encourage Christian schools to hire believers with a genuine relationship with Christ.

Conclusion

In this chapter, we have examined seven principles for assisting educators in Christian schools and student pastors in local churches to integrate the Bible into their education program. Regardless of the institution, integrating the Bible into one's education program well requires careful planning, critical thinking, humble collaboration, vision and mission alignment, and hard work, among other factors. Most importantly, integrating the Bible requires Christian educators and student pastors to value Scripture as the most essential tool for preparing Christian disciples who love, trust, and obey Christ.[13]

---

[13] Special thanks to Dr. Bobby Howard (SCBC), Josh Forrest (Columbia First Baptist, Columbia, SC), and Dr. Matt Harrison (Grace Baptist Church, Knoxville, TN) for reviewing the draft of this chapter.

CHAPTER 14

RESPONDING TO A CRISIS IN A MODERN STUDENT: STRATEGY AND TOOLS FOR "WHAT DO I DO WHEN?"

Ron Harvell, D.Min.

Blessed be the God and Father of our Lord Jesus Christ, the Father of mercies and God of all comfort, who comforts us in all our affliction, so that we may be able to comfort those who are in any affliction, with the comfort with which we ourselves are comforted by God (2 Corinthians 1:3-4, ESV).

He was sitting on the faculty's supply closet floor when one of the administrative assistants found him. He said, "It's okay for me to be here since my daddy was a teacher. It was a long time ago, before he left us, before he wrecked us. Oh, Daddy!"

Thank you for leading your youth and students to journey with the Lord. So many important and eternal things are taking place in their lives. You may have a long history of helping youth and students deal with significant issues in their lives. You may be new to the front lines of caring for them in crisis. Regardless of your experience level, I encourage you to think through possible scenarios and ask, "What do I do when something happens?" Then think about, "How can I help prevent these things from happening?"

The need for modern teenagers to have people intersect their lives for good is extraordinary. In the United States, teenagers are much more likely than adults to visit a mental health counselor, take mental health medication, and have more exaggerated moods than those over 18. Severity of mental health-related concerns will be very individualized.[1]

In the United States, an average person will experience two to three traumatic events during their lifetime. By the age of 18, many will have experienced some form of significant trauma. A first responder in a large city will see 200 or more very traumatic events in a 20-year career.[2] While the average person's traumatic events are low compared to those of first responders, medical personnel, and relief workers, a lower-level crisis is common and significant.

Students and youth may be in great anxiety about simple to complex issues. This can range from getting a B+ instead of an A, rejection by a boyfriend, the tsunami of divorce, being abused, or the news of the death of a friend.

In the spiritual warfare arena, Satan desires to hurt God by hurting people. Satan sells doubt, shame, worthlessness, loneliness, and insecurity as the sand upon which he wants your students to build their lives. You offer a better and greater way.

Increasing your crisis care skills equips you to serve others better. Increasing your viewpoint on crisis care gives a strategic way to see the value of your work. This strategic perspective helps you lead and

---

[1] National Alliance on Mental Health, "Mental Health By the Numbers." NAMI. Retrieved 17 May, 2022 from https://www.nami.org/mhstats.

[2] Luther Rice, Chief of Police, Charleston, South Carolina, "The Value of Chaplains for Police Officers" (Lecture, Dewey Center for Chaplaincy, Introduction to Crisis Ministry, Zoom conference, Charleston Southern University, January 27, 2021).

care through *prevention, intervention,* and *reinvention.* These three areas help you prevent crisis, care for those in immediate need, and enable people to grow after their crisis.

Prevention – Hope is the Strategy

Hope is the outcome of faith. Hope prevents many crises from happening or worsening. Hope is the greatest shield for people who experience and endure a crisis. Hope comes from purpose, worth, and community. These are God's gifts to people to trust Him for both today and tomorrow. Prior to a crisis, you can develop these qualities in your students. You and the Lord can build a rock-solid foundation for them so they can prevent many crises and endure other crises. They can know God wants to walk with them through the storms.

> Everyone then who hears these words of mine and does them will be like a wise man who built his house on the rock. And the rain fell, and the floods came, and the winds blew and beat on that house, but it did not fall, because it had been founded on the rock. And everyone who hears these words of mine and does not do them will be like a foolish man who built his house on the sand. And the rain fell, and the floods came, and the winds blew and beat against that house, and it fell, and great was the fall of it (Matthew 7:24-27, ESV).

Hope is the strategy. It is important to be *Left of the Bang.* This is a military term for getting ahead of the enemy and preventing conflict. It is wise to invest in prevention and preparation for life. Build in your students' lives Jesus and His Word. If they build well, then many crises can be lessened or avoided.

God calls us to care for and build up one another. Based upon research from Duke and Harvard Universities, in 2016 the United States Air Force Chaplain's Corps built a campaign entitled "Faith Works." The results of these studies validated the importance of having a faith and practicing that faith with others. The measure of one's faith practiced with others is called *religiosity*. Religiosity measures the positive outcomes of a faith practiced with other people.

Thinking of prevention, here is an example from hundreds of studies that Harvard (public health) and Duke (mental health) ran or validated. In a Harvard study of 90,000 nurses over 15 years, those who practiced their faith with others once a week were five times less likely to have suicidal ideations, attempts, or successful tries.[3] The current US completed suicide rate is 48,000 a year, 132 a day, and 13.4 suicides per 1000.[4] If everyone practiced their faith with others, a fivefold decrease would be possible—2.7 people per 1,000 or 26 people a day rather than 132 people a day. If everyone practiced their faith with others, the rate could be 38,400 fewer suicides per year. Encouraging your teenagers to attend church at least weekly will result in significant positive outcomes in their lives.

And let us consider how to stir up one another to love and good works, not neglecting to meet together, as is the habit of some, but encouraging one another, and all the more as you see the Day drawing near (Hebrews 10:24-25, ESV).

God wants your students to have abundant life. At the Pentagon, I was privileged to work on a task force for suicide and violence prevention. As a chaplain and general officer, the Lord opened many doors for increasing the value of faith in helping change people's lives.

While there, I developed a way of looking at one's faith in relation to other disciplines. The domains of mental, physical, and social health are of great value to us, but the spiritual domain has even greater value since it is the core of who people are. All four domains are dynamic. What we do and think directly correlates to our lives.

---

[3] VanderWeele, T. J. (2017). "On the promotion of human flourishing." Proceedings of the National Academy of Sciences, 114(31), 8148–8156. Https://www.pnas.org/doi/full/10.1073/pnas.1702996114.

[4] Center for Disease Control, "Suicide Prevention," CDC. Retrieved 6 June, 2022 from https://www.cdc.gov/suicide.

Each of these domains have the capability to be exercised. With the right kind of effort and exercise, one can increase their fitness.

Physical fitness is measured by physicality.

Mental fitness is measured by mentality.

Social fitness is measured by sociality.

Spiritual fitness is measured by spirituality.

The amount of investment in each category can provide evidence of effort and its effects. It is arguable to say that spirituality is at the center of a person and is the most important sphere. A person's spiritual fitness is worth noticing and increasing. Consider engaging your teenagers with an assessment or inventory to see where they are in their spiritual journey. The most important assessment of a Christian school is whether the level of faith of individual students is increasing or decreasing. Disciple well.

As you model, teach, and project worth, community, and purpose you build prevention's muscles. You exercise the lane of soul care by being a godly model of a Christian. You value biblical marriage, avoiding sexual sin, not participating in pornography, not abusing others, going to church with family or friends, maintaining a daily walk with the Lord, and striving to serve others with no ulterior motives.

As you think about prevention, encourage parents to engage their children, fostering beliefs and behaviors which support their children's spiritual development. Dr. Tyler VanderWeele of Harvard University, the world's leading public health researcher, states that the number one predictor of poverty in America is homes where the father is not present.[5] Encourage families to work to make it work. Teach students how to break the cycle of sin in their families. The greatest investment in student development is encouraging families to stay together.

---

[5] VanderWeele, T. J. (2017). "On the promotion of human flourishing." Proceedings of the National Academy of Sciences, 114(31), 8148–8156. Https://www.pnas.org/doi/full/10.1073/pnas.1702996114.

Marriage promotes greater satisfaction and happiness, mental and physical health, meaning and purpose, and many other positive outcomes. Children of parents who stay together will have children who benefit from these positive marriage effects. They are also more likely to marry and not divorce. They, too, have better mental and physical health, are less likely to engage in delinquent and criminal behaviors and are more likely to have good relationships with their parents. When parents commit to remain together the positive consequences of flourishing are dramatic for the family.

Marriage has profound positives that are seen as great negatives when a divorce takes place. Poorer mental health, physical health, less happiness and satisfaction, lower sense of meaning and purpose, poorer relationships between children and parents, and greater poverty for children and mothers. Dr. VanderWeele said, "The miracle cure for American Society is for fathers and mothers to stay together."[6]

A life built upon the rock has hope. It is the strategy and goal of prevention. This is the daily journey in the life-long journey of caring for your students, youth, and yourself. But storms come.

Intervention – The Holy Spirit is the Key

Do nothing out of selfish ambition or vain conceit. Rather, in humility value others above yourselves, not looking to your own interests but each of you to the interests of the others (Philippians 2:3-4, NIV).

Intervention is an action toward helping people. Trusting in the Holy Spirit is key for intervention to work. Intervention is vitally needed in the lives of people throughout the world. Ask the Lord to build you up since the need is so great. The World Health Organiza-

---

[6] VanderWeele, T. J. (2017). "On the promotion of human flourishing." Proceedings of the National Academy of Sciences, 114(31), 8148–8156. Https://www.pnas.org/doi/full/10.1073/pnas.1702996114.

tion, in March of 2022,[7] saw a 25% increase in anxiety and depression following COVID-19 global pandemic. National adult mental health[8] rates show 1 out of 5 are dealing with mental health issues; this is higher in adolescents.

LivingWorks[9] identifies that 1 out of 25 people are thinking about suicide. Awareness is important in any level of care, particularly in intervention. According to LivingWorks,[10] people often give indicators or have circumstances that reflect a change in their lives. It is easy to miss, dismiss, or avoid warning signals people give. Noticing changes in a person's life is often the beginning of recognizing the need for intervention. When you or another person notice a change in someone's behavior, ask how they are doing.[11]

Awareness is important. There should be no safer place for children than in your homes, church buildings, and schools. I know a girl who was bullied so severely in school that she ate her lunch in fear every day on a toilet in the girls' restroom. Twenty years later, she is still traumatized by that experience. How is it that cafeteria workers, administrators, maintenance staff, teachers, parents, and students were not aware enough to rescue her? What did they miss, dismiss, or avoid?[12] One of prevention's greatest skills and the first step in intervention is noticing a change in someone's life.

---

[7] World Health Organization. "Covid-19 pandemic triggers 25% increase in prevalence of anxiety and depression worldwide." World Health Organization. Retrieved 2 March 2022 from https://www.who.int/news/item/02-03-2022-covid-19-pandemic-triggers-25-increase-in-prevalence-of-anxiety-and-depression-worldwide.

[8] National Alliance on Mental Health. "Mental Health By the Numbers." Retrieved 17 May, 2022 from https://www.nami.org/mhstats.

[9] LivingWorks. "Why Suicide Prevention Matters." Retrieved 15 June, 2022 from https://www.livingworks.net/why-suicide-prevention-matters.

[10] LivingWorks. "Why Suicide Prevention Matters." Miss, dismiss, and avoid are three categories where awareness needs to be increased.

[11] LivingWorks. "Why Suicide Prevention Matters." Retrieved 15 June, 2022 from https://www.livingworks.net/why-suicide-prevention-matters.

[12] LivingWorks SafeTALK. Often we miss the "tells" or signs of a person in distress by missing, dismissing, or avoiding ways to help them.

Ask the Lord to help you care for others, empowered by the Holy Spirit. Become a prayer warrior for your students and your community. Ask the Lord to overflow you with His Spirit.[13]

> If you ask me anything in my name, I will do it. "If you love me, you will keep my commandments. And I will ask the Father, and he will give you another Helper, to be with you forever, even the Spirit of truth, whom the world cannot receive, because it neither sees him nor knows him. You know him, for he dwells with you and will be in you. "I will not leave you as orphans; I will come to you" (John 14:14-18, ESV).

As you think about intervention, have resources ready to help you engage someone. In addition to being prepared spiritually, use the following to prepare logistically to care for your teens and students.

1. What are my organization's policies on intervention?
   - At your school, what are the processes for seeking help, permission, etc.?
   - Has the school discussed these policies and processes with the entire staff?
   - What are the roles for emergencies?
   - If the school has a counselor, what are his or her policies?
   - What about after hours or emergencies?
   - What are the emergency contact numbers?
2. If after hours, what variables apply? Discuss with your leadership team the best ways to help someone:
   - On campus or off?
   - Field trips?

---

[13] Rob Dewey, "Underneath the Ravanel Bridge" (Lecture, The Dewey Center for Chaplaincy, Introduction to Crisis Ministry, January 19, 2021). Rob was the direct family minister to a man who hurt 100's of women. The evil of this person was so great that Rob needed friends to pray with him to be free from the thought He needed to be filled and overflowing with the Holy Spirit. "Evil is real. The Holy Spirit is greater."

- Overnights?
3. Build a contact list of people you trust and can resource as needed for each circumstance. Below is a sample contact form titled "My Intervention Contact List." Think about different scenarios and who would be best to talk with the student or students. This could be counselors, ministers, medical personnel, etc.

My Intervention Contact List			
Category	**Name**	**Number**	**Other Contact Info**
Local Emergency #s			
Principle			
School Counselor			
Church Pastor			
Emergency Room			
Counselor			
Crisis Conversation	Disaster Distress Helpline TTY for Deaf/Hearing Impaired	1-800-985-5990 TTY: 800-846-8517	Text 66746
Child Abuse		1-800-442-4453	
988 Suicide and and Crisis Lifeline		Call or text 988	988lifeline.org
National Sexual Human Trafficing	CAST	1-800-656-4673 888-539-2373	www.rainn.org
Other			

My Class Contact			
This is for you to have the ability to contact student/family during an emergency.			
Name:	Number	Address:	Email:
Parent:			
Student:			

4. Develop your own "My Class Contacts" list of parents and students. Have contact lists for after-hours communication as need.

When the Intervention Begins

Step 1 – Remember to pray for the Holy Spirit's Leadership.

Seek the Holy Spirit to fill you to overflowing, to help you be in-step with Him, and to bear the fruit of the Spirit—Love, Joy, Peace, Patience, Kindness, Goodness, Faithfulness, Gentleness, and Self-Control (Galatians 5:22-23).[14]

Step 2 – Release your control of the situation and ask the Lord to give you the wisdom to be in tune with Him.

> If any of you lacks wisdom, let him ask God, who gives generously to all without reproach, and it will be given him. But let him ask in faith, with no doubting, for the one who doubts is like a wave of the sea that is driven and tossed by the wind. For that person must not suppose that he will receive anything from the Lord; he is a double-minded man, unstable in all his ways (James 1:5-8, ESV).

Step 3 – Thank God that He has asked you to help in this ministry of intervention

Key things to think about and do:

- Be aware of those involved

Some crisis intervention is very private and may only involve one person. Sometimes many are involved. Note who might need support.

---

[14] Rob Dewey, "Underneath the Ravanel Bridge" (Lecture, The Dewey Center for Chaplaincy, Introduction to Crisis Ministry, January 19, 2021). "Evil is real. The Holy Spirit is greater."

- Be aware of the location

  Where do you need to be? If you are going to a hospital, jail, military base, school, or home, having information about entry will be helpful.

- Be able to listen to concerns

  Listening is one of the intervention's most valuable skills. Listening allows the person in need to share their concerns. Listening is often equated with caring. We can presume many things about a person prior to talking with them. Once you really listen you get a clearer picture of their concerns.

- Be courageously humble and confident in God

  God walks with you as you walk with others.

- Be able to speak as led by Holy Spirit

  Some may fear saying the wrong thing to a person in crisis. When you care about others and listen to the Lord, have confidence God will speak through you. World-famous first responder chaplain Rev. Rob Dewey talked over 200 people from jumping off bridges. In most of his thousands of interventions, he started the conversation by asking, "How can I help you?"

If someone is not acting like themselves, a direct conversation is important. They may be having a bad day. They may be suicidal. You need to listen to them and then discuss what is going on. I encourage you to be bold in your questions if you think they might be suicidal. Here is a simple way to ask and a framework that LivingWorks uses. You will fill in the two or three things they have shown you or you observe that raised your concerns and then ask the important question. "Sometimes people who are not acting like themselves have experienced a difficult loss, and have stopped coming to class are thinking about suicide. Are you thinking about suicide?"[15]

---

[15] SafeTALK, "Miss, Dismiss, Avoid." From Dr. Harvell, "Over the past few months, we have had three suicide interventions by three people who recently took our SafeTALK suicide awareness program. One a student with a student, one a staff member with a student, one

Even if they are not thinking about suicide, they are displaying that something is different, so ask how you can help.

- Share a prayer or read the Bible as led

  The Bible and prayer are vital to spiritual growth. If I do not know the person or family well, I will wait for a while and at an appropriate time ask if I could read from the Bible and pray for them. Most say yes.

- Pray as the Holy Spirit leads you.

- Read the Bible as the Holy Spirit leads you.

Psalm 23 is a powerful Bible passage for those who are hurting. Here are ten more great Bible verses to have on your phone or contact list from Debbie McDaniel's, "10 Bible Verses for Tough Times."[16]

1. "He heals the brokenhearted and binds up their wounds" (Psalm 147:3, ESV).

2. "The LORD is near to the brokenhearted and saves the crushed in spirit" (Psalm 34:18, ESV).

3. "But he gives more grace. Therefore it says, 'God opposes the proud, but gives grace to the humble'" (James 4:6, ESV).

4. "I believe that I shall look upon the goodness of the LORD in the land of the living! Wait for the LORD; be strong, and let your heart take courage; wait for the LORD!" (Psalm 27:13-14, ESV).

5. "Blessed be God, the Father of our Lord Jesus Christ, the Father of mercies, and God of all comfort, who comforts us in all our affliction, so that we may be able to comfort those who are in any affliction, with the comfort with which we ourselves are comforted by God" (2 Corinthians 1:3-4, ESV).

---

a lay person from a local church with another parishioner. All three used what they had learned."

[16] Debbie McDaniel. Crosswalk.com. "Prayer and Bible Verses for Comfort When You're Hurting in Tough Times." Retrieved 8 July, 2016 from https://www.crosswalk.com/blogs/debbie-mcdaniel/a-prayer-for-when-youre-hurting-10-verses-of-comfort-for-tough-times.html.

6. "Fear not, for I am with you; do not be dismayed, for I am your God; I will strengthen you, I will help you, I will uphold you with My righteous right hand" (Isaiah 41:10, ESV).

7. "He himself bore our sins in his body on the tree, that we might die to sin and live to righteousness. By his wounds, you have been healed" (1 Peter 2:24, ESV).

8. "Cast your burden on the LORD, and he will sustain you; he will never permit the righteous to be moved" (Psalm 55:22, ESV).

9. "Come to me, all who labor and are heavy laden, and I will give you rest. Take my yoke upon you, and learn from me, for I am gentle and lowly in heart, and you will find rest for your souls. For my yoke is easy, and my burden is light" (Matthew 11:28-30, ESV).

10. "But he said to me, 'My grace is sufficient for you, for my power is made perfect in weakness.' Therefore I will boast all the more gladly of my weaknesses, so that the power of Christ may rest upon me" (2 Corinthians 12:9, ESV).

Reinvention – Having an Eternal Perspective

"But he said to me, 'My grace is sufficient for you, for my power is made perfect in weakness.' Therefore I will boast all the more gladly of my weaknesses, so that the power of Christ may rest upon me" (2 Corinthians 12:9, ESV).

The storm has come, and it is time to rebuild lives and community. Some call this last step in the continuum of care postvention,[17] but I refer to it as reinvention. The intervention was a divine appointment with you and the person or people in crisis. Having this same kind of care for their future is crucial for the success of their recovery. The nature of the crisis will determine the complexity of the reinvention.

Most people need to heal and grieve from a crisis. God's next steps will help you move them into reinvention with Him. As a be-

---

[17] Continuum of Care is a phrase used for an intentional effort to help people after a crisis.

liever, many will naturally look to you as God's ambassador in the situation. God called you to be the divine presence in their recovery.

God's ultimate outcome for their lives is to grow in their faith, knowing the Lord as Savior and established in Him. God brought you into their lives to help make an eternal difference. God is working in their lives to comfort them and use this situation for good. Have an eternal mindset that the Lord is at work in the lives of people, drawing them to Himself. Therefore, seek the Lord for His paths and purpose in their lives. Develop a growth plan with God's help and the people involved. (See chart below)

Explore the faith of the families to see where they are. Find out who they know who can help them recover and journey with them. This includes family, pastors, medical experts, counselors, churches, and helping organizations.

Sometimes the crisis involves the death of a student from your school, a youth from church, or one of their family members. You may be invited to be a part of a memorial service, funeral, or wake. The person or people may have died of natural causes or an accident or suicide. Here are some tips for these kinds of services.

Tips for memorial services, funerals, wakes:

- 150–300 people can be affected by a suicide, car accident, overdose, etc.
- Don't glorify self-harm consequences.
- Don't say things that were not true about the person.
- Honor their family.
- Honor God and talk about eternal things.

Hopelessness is a leading indicator of suicide risk.[18] In these times students will be thinking about life and death issues. Addressing

---

[18] Ed Praetorian, "Mental Health Training and Intervention: A Critical Component of Police Reform," Survey: "What is the state of officer mental health in 2020?" Mr. Michelle Lilly and Sergeant Shawn Curry, Scribd, September 14, 2020, https://www.police1.com/health-wellness/articles/survey-what-is-the-state-of-officer-mental-health-in-2020-oXldKxzNnuebFluY/.

these issues is valuable. Helping people know the Lord, is the most valuable.

- Develop resources from their family and community who can help those in greatest need.

Design a contact list that has many of the resources on the "My Intervention Contact List." This list will focus on recovery and reinvention, helping others grow past the storm and come out stronger.

Reinvention Paths		
Helping People Grow Closer to God After a Crisis		
Topic	**Date**	**Contact Information**
Initial Meetings after Crisis		
Follow-up on progress		
Contact lists for families and churches to connect		
Pastor		
Counselor		
Spiritual Growth Plan		
Faith		
Salvation		
Parents/Family		
Connections for follow-up		
Event Baptism		
Grief Group		
Collaborate with Co-Workers		

Conclusion

Thank you again for your ministries. Be courageous and trust in God. The modern teenager needs Jesus to be the center of their lives. They need their Abba Father. God wants you to help continue to build their lives upon the Rock. They need their Abba Father. God sometimes calls you to be with them in the storms.

They need their Abba Father. God chooses you to be in the journey of their recovery and reinvention.

> And let us not grow weary of doing good, for in due season we will reap, if we do not give up. So then, as we have opportunity, let us do good to everyone, and especially to those who are of the household of faith (Galatians 6:9-10, ESV).

No longer abandoned on the floor of a supply closet.

No longer drowning in a pool of tears in a desperate search for a missing father.

Here is the Daddy who never leaves you.

Here is the Daddy who is with you as you grow.

Here is the Daddy who is with you as you hurt.

Here is the Daddy who is with you forever.

"Oh, Daddy! Thank you! Oh, Daddy, I love you! Oh, Daddy!"

CONCLUSION

At the conclusion of his gospel, John writes, "Now Jesus did many other signs in the presence of the disciples, which are not written in this book; but these are written so that you may believe that Jesus is the Christ, the Son of God, and that by believing you may have life in his name" (John 20:30-31 ESV). Our prayer is that this work has helped you see the beauty of the reliability, authority, and message of our Ancient Text and the life that it can give students today. We also hope that you understand better the modern world students are living in and how the Ancient Text still speaks to a modern audience. We also hope this work has given you some new practical helps based on the Ancient Text in your ministries, small groups, and classrooms to better disciple your modern students. Our ultimate prayer is that in all our ministries students will "believe that Jesus is the Christ, the Son of God" and they would have "life in His name."

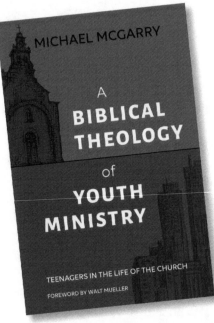

A Biblical Theology of Youth Ministry

Teenagers in the Life of the Church

by Michael McGarry, D.Min.

ISBN: 9781614840961 Price: $19.99

WWW.RANDALLHOUSE.COM • 1-800-877-7030

RANDALL HOUSE
— ACADEMIC —

Southwestern
BAPTIST THEOLOGICAL SEMINARY

D6
FAMILY MINISTRY
Journal

D6 Family Ministry Journals Volumes 1-5

The purpose of the *Southwestern D6 Family Ministry Journal* is to support the thinking and practices of parenting in Christian homes, in family ministry in the local church, and in parachurch settings that reflect God's intent for generational discipleship as presented in Deuteronomy 6 and other biblical texts. This purpose is achieved by the publication of academic peer-reviewed articles along with a limited selection of practitioner insights and book reviews on recent family ministry titles. The journal is primarily intended for two audiences: (1) an academic community of professors and students in institutions of higher learning who are committed to the development of a new generation of Christian ministers and community leaders and (2) those professionals who are already serving in local church and parachurch settings. The Journal hopes to facilitate discussion and learning among both groups.

🏛 **www.D6family.com/D6academic** \\ **1.800.877.7030**